In a world where technology is advancing faster than ever, the real challenge is not simply adopting new tools, but enabling people and organizations to adapt with clarity, confidence, and purpose. Brent Snyder and David Kramer provide an insightful and practical framework that helps leaders move beyond traditional digital transformation toward true digital enablement—aligning people, processes, technology, and data to create lasting value in an increasingly automated economy.

Stephen M. R. Covey,
The New York Times and #1 *Wall Street Journal*
bestselling author of *The Speed of Trust* and *Trust & Inspire*

DIGITAL
ENABLEMENT

DIGITAL ENABLEMENT

HOW HIGH-PERFORMING COMPANIES ARE DOMINATING THE AUTOMATED ECONOMY

BRENT SNYDER **DAVID KRAMER**

RESULTS FASTER!
PUBLISHING

Digital Enablement: How High-Performing Companies Are Dominating The Automated Economy

Published by *RESULTS Faster!* Publishing in Flower Mound, TX

Printed in the United States of America

CONTENTS

FOREWORD by Tony Jeary xi

OVERVIEW FOR DIGITAL ENABLEMENT
You Can't Even See It xv

PART ONE Macro Disruptions 1

PART TWO The Automated Economy 31

PART THREE Digital Enablement 49

PART FOUR Digital Enablement Call To Action—
Now is the Time to Engage 75

25 Executive Takeaways for Becoming
Digitally Enabled 87

About the Authors 93

About Cooperative Computing 97

FOREWORD
by Tony Jeary

For decades, we've helped companies grow and scale. At the RESULTS Center, our specialty is helping organizations get clear, get focused, and execute, fast. In fact, our company's proven methodology is built around those three words. We take leaders' visions and help them turn them into reality faster.

When we begin a relationship with a growing organization that wants to keep accelerating, we almost always start with an assessment of ten areas where leaders can grade themselves to determine the obvious areas of focus. Those areas include customer experience, marketing, sales, finance, operations, culture, and—of course, in today's rapidly changing world—digital maturity.

The first nine are usually expected. But when we get to the tenth—digital—leaders pause. They take a breath, nod slowly, and say something like, "That's where we need help." How about you? Chances are you're reading this foreword because the title caught your eye, and you're ready to figure out how to catch up, keep up, and truly leverage technology in your business.

The truth is, most organizations are like the battleship in the story you'll read at the start of this book—trying to command the immovable to move. Digital Enablement is how you adjust your course.

Brent Snyder and David Kramer are longtime friends, and we often introduce them to our clients because they see what others can't. They understand how to bring clarity and practicality to the complex world of digital transformation. They help leaders course-correct before it's too late—and turn disruption into opportunity.

This book is both an insurance policy and an invitation. It will help you see the digital frontier clearly and motivate you to take action. You'll discover not just what's changing, but how to navigate, adapt, and thrive in an age where technology and clarity drive results.

Enjoy the journey.

Tony Jeary—The RESULTS Guy™

OVERVIEW FOR DIGITAL ENABLEMENT

YOU CAN'T EVEN SEE IT

Your plan is failing, and you need a new plan.

Take a moment and imagine the year 2035.

Eighty percent of the enterprises of today will be irrelevant.

The pace at which buyers expect products, services and experiences has shifted business into a constant state of acceleration. Business models have shifted at a rapid pace, making your business model obsolete. Markets no longer reward size alone. They reward speed, clarity, and alignment. Organizations that fail to adapt do not disappear overnight. They fall behind incrementally, until relevance erodes. The companies that succeed must be agile, adaptable and aggressively innovative.

Every outcome in this environment begins the same way. Every action is preceded by thought. Decisions are not reactions to reality. They are interpretations of it. Organizations perform in direct proportion to how their leaders see the world. When thinking aligns with reality, execution compounds. When thinking lags reality, friction grows and performance slows—often without obvious warning.

ELEVATE YOUR THINKING

There is a story that captures this dynamic with precision (first published by Frank Koch in the Naval Institute Magazine *Proceedings*).

> Two battleships assigned to the training squadron had been at sea on maneuvers in heavy weather for several days. I was serving on the lead battleship and was on watch on the bridge as night fell. The visibility was poor with patchy fog, so the captain remained on the bridge keeping an eye on all activities.
>
> Shortly after dark, the lookout on the wing of the bridge reported, "Light, bearing on the starboard bow."
>
> "Is it steady or moving astern?" the captain called out.
>
> Lookout replied, "Steady, Captain," which meant we were on a dangerous collision course with that ship.
>
> The captain then called to the signalman, "Signal that ship: We are on a collision course; advise you change course 20 degrees."
>
> Back came a signal, "Advisable for you to change course 20 degrees."

The captain said, "Send, I'm a captain, change course 20 degrees."

"I'm a seaman second class," came the reply. "You had better change course 20 degrees."

By that time, the captain was furious. He spat out, "Send, I'm a battleship. Change course 20 degrees."

Back came the flashing light, "I'm a lighthouse."

We changed course.

The story endures because it exposes a structural truth. Authority does not alter reality. Experience does not override it. Confidence does not move it. The lighthouse does not negotiate. The only variable that changes is the assumption held by the one approaching it.

This is how paradigms operate.

Paradigms are not careless errors. They are frameworks built from experience. They are shaped by upbringing, family, environment, education, culture, and professional success. Over time, these influences form perspectives. Perspectives become habitual. Habits of thought harden into operating assumptions. Eventually, they function invisibly.

Consider a few examples of our own lives, our parents, our upbringing, where we lived, where we went to school, who we hung around with, and the very life experiences we have had interacting with others. These very experiences shape our perspectives for how we view the world, and therefore, lead to our actions. What if these perspectives are not always accurate?

The danger is not that paradigms exist. The danger is that they remain unexamined.

As paradigms settle into the background, leaders stop seeing them. Decisions feel rational. Actions feel justified. Yet outcomes increasingly fail to match intent. Not because effort declines, but because the underlying view of reality no longer fits the environment being navigated.

Your plan is failing and you don't know it yet. Your dashboards look healthy. Your teams are executing. Your forecasts still hold. But beneath the surface, something is breaking. Your customers are comparing you to companies you don't even consider competitors. Your decision cycles are slower than the market you operate in. Your systems are creating friction your leadership team cannot see. This is how irrelevance begins: not as a collapse, but as a delay.

This matters because thinking always comes first. Every strategy, structure, investment, and priority is downstream from an assumption about how the world works. When those assumptions are incomplete, execution compounds error just as efficiently as it compounds success.

As we begin in this book, we ask you to consider how your thinking has influenced various decisions; in your life, in your family, in your leadership at various times. Please know, undoubtedly, your thinking has been shaped by various elements, whether this be your upbringing, your education, the different types of people you have interacted with or simply where you are from; each of these may have varying degrees of influence in how you think. And every action we take comes directly from the thoughts we have. So the question is not *whether leaders are capable or disciplined;* it is *whether the thinking that produced past results is sufficient for the environment now unfold-*

ing. As you read *Digital Enablement,* we invite you to elevate your thinking and consider where we might go together in accelerating into the automated economy. Because the economy has changed, legacy thought leadership needs to shift.

"Legacy Thought Leadership" is the condition in which executive teams are still leading the enterprise through assumptions, management habits, and operating models shaped by a prior era of business. These leaders are often highly capable and deeply experienced, but the perspective guiding the organization was built for a world with less complexity, fewer choices, slower change and more clearly separated functions. As a result, leadership thinking often remains centered on organizational silos, legacy methods and procedures, disconnected systems and technologies, and metrics that measure functional activity more than enterprise performance. What makes this "legacy" is not the age of the leaders, but the age of the leadership model itself. It reflects a way of seeing the business that no longer fully matches the speed, connectivity, and intelligence now required to compete and grow.

In practical terms, Legacy Thought Leadership limits a leadership teams ability to create a new perspective across the five key business segments of the enterprise: branding and marketing, sales and commerce, operations and fulfillment (including finance and accounting), customer engagement and service delivery. Instead of seeing these segments as interconnected parts of one economic system, they are often managed as separate domains with separate priorities, separate technologies and separate measures of success. That fragmentation slows digital enablement, weakens decision-making, and makes it harder for leaders to drive Hyper-automation, Hyper-personalization, and Data-driven decisions across the enterprise. In this sense, Legacy Thought Leadership is one of the greatest barriers to preparing the modern enterprise for the Automated Economy, because it prevents leaders from adopting the integrated, forward-looking perspective required to align the business, modernize execution and lead with greater clarity in a rapidly changing world.

In this book we seek to help leaders shift their **Legacy Thought Leadership** so they can see the art of possible, reduce the risk of failure and gain practical insight into the digital frontier. We introduce the **Automated Economy** and show how **Digital Enablement**—the deliberate alignment of people, processes, systems, and data—unifies an enterprise so it can operate at the speed today's Automated Economy demands, helping to create a self-optimizing enterprise capable of hypergrowth.

We establish a clear, durable framework for understanding how enterprises such as yours must adapt in response to timeless buyer behavior, the accelerating automation of the global economy, and the macro disruptions reshaping every industry.

While the technologies of each era change, the underlying principles of governing value creation, delivery, and consumption remain remarkably consistent.

Digital Enablement is grounded in these principles and provides leaders with a practical lens for helping navigate the next phase of economic transformation. At its core, Digital Enablement is the bridge between the world as it is and the Automated Economy now emerging.

Being challenged by growth, risk-taking, and innovation in the modern era requires a digitally enabled foundation. **Organizations that fail to evolve will be made irrelevant by the Automated Economy rather than participating in it.**

UNDERSTANDING BUYER OBSESSION

The term "**Buyer Obsession**" defines a simple reality: since the beginning of time, buyers have wanted what they want, when they want it, at the value they want it. This simple statement captures a timeless and immutable truth that transcends geography, industry, and technological era. Whether in ancient trade markets, industrial supply chains, or modern digital ecosystems, buyer behavior has consistently exerted pressure on organizations to reduce friction, increase availability, and optimize value.

All economic systems, business models and technologies ultimately exist to serve this core demand. **As buyer expectations increase, organizations are compelled to respond by improving speed, reducing cost, increasing choice, and delivering experiences that feel increasingly personalized and effortless.** Understanding this foundational principle is essential, because every subsequent shift in the economy is, at its core, a response to this enduring buyer demand, the obsession.

Every era of economic development has carried with it a dominant myth—the belief that producers, inventors, and capital holders shape the destiny of commerce. But beneath every empire built, every market formed, and every system of exchange perfected, there has always existed a quieter, far more consistent force: the will of the buyer.

Buyer behavior has always expressed itself in the same way. Buyers want what they want. They want it when they want it. And they want it at the value they are willing to pay. These expectations are not trends. They are the baseline against which all economic activity is measured. What has changed is the speed at which these expectations assert themselves.

Buyers—whether individuals seeking comfort, merchants pursuing profit, or institutions managing scarcity—have always been the architects of economic motion. The buyer is in charge.

At its core, Digital Enablement is the bridge between the world as it is and the Automated Economy now emerging.

Not executives. Not organizations. Not technology. The buyer decides what is valuable, what scales, and what survives. Producers do not create demand; they interpret it. Governments do not invent markets; they regulate what buyers have already established.

In the book by Adam Smith, *The Wealth of Nations,* he makes reference to the invisible hand guiding the market. He was not referring to governments, corporations, or entrepreneurs. He was describing the aggregated psychology of countless buyers making choices—the true invisible engine of the global economy.

As buyer expectations accelerate, organizations built on slow decision cycles, fragmented systems and rigid hierarchies struggle to respond. This is often misinterpreted as a technology gap. It is not. It is a structural and cognitive gap. Technology simply exposes it.

Executives who understand the buyer is the economy unlock a fundamentally different approach to growth strategy. In traditional thinking, the enterprise competes by optimizing production or market share. In the age of automation, it competes by enabling the buyer's journey more completely than anyone else.

This shift from optimizing market share to optimizing the buyers journey requires three realizations:

1. Economic growth is behavioral, not mechanical.
2. Innovation is no longer invention—it is orchestration.
3. Leadership must evolve from control to enablement.

At the center of every disruption is buyer obsession. This obsession provides opportunity and drives a cycle of innovators, adopters and implementers.

Innovators are driving innovation across production, distribution, and acquisition simultaneously. Someone recognizes an unmet buyer desire and creates a way to fulfill it. These innovators introduce a promise into the market. As the promise proves valuable, others repeat it.

Adopters expand availability and increase buyer quantity. Markets begin to form. Competition intensifies. As volume grows, implementation replaces experimentation.

Implementers scale delivery, standardize fulfillment, and expand reach.

As promises scale, enablement becomes unavoidable. Choices alone are no longer sufficient. Choices must converge with the ability to deliver faster, more efficiently, and at greater scale. A choice does not matter until it converges with execution.

The term "Buyer Obsession" defines a simple reality; since the beginning of time, buyers have wanted what they want, when they want it, at the value they want it.

Learning models evolve. Business models adjust. Standards reset. Each cycle tightens the next, compressing time and reducing tolerance for inefficiency.

Every economic interaction begins with desire, not with product or price. That desire may be personal, organizational, or subconscious, but its structure is consistent.

When examined through behavioral economics, consumer psychology and systems theory, all "buyer desire" ultimately expresses itself through three immutable forces:

1. The Need for Specificity—"I want what I want."
2. The Demand for Immediacy—"I want it when I want it."
3. The Expectation of Value—"I want it at the value I want it."

Enterprises must be designed to sense and respond to these forces in real time. Oftentimes, you can't even see it. Organizations have been talking themselves out of making changes for decades. This is not a theoretical distinction; this is operational. The capability to do so is Digital Enablement.

Digital Enablement is the deliberate alignment of people, processes, systems and data so an enterprise can operate at the speed desired by buyers in the Automated Economy. It operationalizes Hyper-automation, Hyper-personalization and Data-driven decision making so the enterprise can scale the delivery of its promise as buyer demand expands.

This book exists because many organizations are still operating with legacy thinking in an environment that no longer rewards it. Leadership models designed for stability are colliding with markets that demand speed. Decision structures built for control are slowing execution. Systems optimized for reporting are failing to support action.

The result is not a lack of intelligence or ambition. It is misalignment.

If you are leading a $50+ million enterprise or operating inside one several times that size, you already feel this pressure. Growth becomes harder to sustain. Complexity increases as organizations scale. Visibility diminishes. Despite greater effort, results take longer to achieve.

Leaders respond by seeking perspective. Coaches are hired. Peer groups are joined. Conferences are attended. The objective is clarity to avoid the unseen lighthouse.

Yet across industries, a consistent realization emerges: Leaders cannot see it.

This is not an anomaly. It is a pattern. Success creates complexity. Complexity obscures reality. The faster the organization grows, the harder it becomes to see friction forming beneath the surface.

As acceleration increases, perspective narrows. Silos form. Decisions fragment. Inefficiency becomes embedded. Peter Drucker captured this reality succinctly when he observed that only three things happen naturally in organizations: confusion, friction and underperformance. Everything else requires leadership.

Digital Enablement provides a leadership framework grounded in realities that have always governed economic motion. Buyer behavior is constant. Macro disruptions are inevitable. The Automated Economy continually evolves. Digital Enablement accelerates through all three.

Ignoring these realities does not slow their impact. It intensifies it.

INTRODUCING TIMELESS TRUTHS

Within Digital Enablement, we identify four primary areas representing timeless principles that help leaders understand where to navigate. These are:

- The **buyer behavior** "is" and has always been the governing force of economic motion
- We experience **Macro Disruptions** that reshape how value is created, delivered and acquired
- The **Automated Economy** continuously evolves as buyer expectations and enterprise capabilities compound
- **Digital Enablement** accelerates through the eras as organizations align people, processes, systems and data

Embracing these four timeless truths is the key to thriving—or getting left behind.

Experiences in recent history makes this clear. How do we handle business during a pandemic? What is the impact of remote work on business? These experiences did not create a new economic condition. They compressed time. They accelerated adoption, expectation, and behavior already in motion. The Automated Economy is the result of compounded acceleration across cycles that once unfolded gradually.

Soon, someone realizes these "buyer behaviors" can be addressed, creates a "commerce" capability to deliver on the want, and provides a CHOICE for the buyer to fulfill the "want." Here in our book, we will simply refer to this group as "innovators"—creating and providing a promise to a select group of buyers.

As buyer demand scales, automation becomes unavoidable. Business models accelerate. Decision cycles compress. Choices multiply. The enterprise either adapts or becomes a constraint. Organizations that thrive pay relentless attention to buyer behavior, deliver faster with less friction, and scale through digitally enabled models.

The number of options available to buyers is increasing at a compound rate. This is the defining condition of the Automated Economy.

The response is not optional. Organizations that fail to evolve will not remain neutral participants. They will be automated by the economy rather than participating in it.

Digital Enablement is the systematic ability to automate, personalize and accelerate decision-making using data—allowing enterprises to exceed buyer expectations at scale. These principles are not new. They are timeless. What feels unprecedented is the speed at which they now assert themselves.

This is not about technology in the old sense of the word. For too long, technology has been placed in the corner of the enterprise, assigned to a department, managed as a support function, and treated as a vertical capability that exists alongside the business rather than within it. In such historical models, technology is something the business "uses," not something that fundamentally reshapes how the business thinks, operates, learns and grows. Such models are now obsolete.

Technology is no longer vertical. It has become horizontal.

What this means is profound. A vertical function lives within a boundary. It has an owner, a budget, a reporting structure, and a defined domain of responsibility. A horizontal capability, by contrast, cuts across every function, every workflow, every decision point, every business unit and every layer of the enterprise. It is embedded in the way branding and marketing engage the market, the way sales and commerce convert demand, the way operations and order fulfillment execute, the way customer engagement and service delivery respond, and the way finance and accounting measure, govern, and guide the enterprise. Once viewed through this lens, technology is no longer merely infrastructure. It becomes the connective tissue of a mature digitally enabled company.

This is why, for us, the better word is not simply "technology," but "digital." Technology often causes leaders to think narrowly—systems, devices, software, infrastructure and IT ownership. Digital causes leaders to think differently. It invites a broader understanding that the enterprise itself must become digitally enabled across its operating model, decision model and learning model. Digital is not confined to applications or platforms. It is the enterprise-wide integration of people, processes, systems, data and actions in ways that remove friction and increase coordinated intelligence across the whole enterprise.

As digital enablement matures, this horizontal nature becomes even more important. In immature enterprises, systems tend to reflect organizational silos. Marketing has its tools. Sales has its tools. Operations has its tools. Finance has its systems of record. Customer service has its platforms. Data is fragmented. Processes are inconsistent. Decisions are delayed. Automation is isolated. Personalization is partial. Reporting is retrospective. In such an environment, each department may improve locally, but the enterprise does not truly accelerate globally. One silo may become more efficient while the company as a whole remains constrained.

This is the central limitation of vertical thinking. It optimizes departments while limiting the performance of the enterprise as a whole.

Horizontal digital enablement changes that. It unifies the enterprise across all business segments so that information, workflows and decisions move with continuity across the business rather than stopping at departmental borders. Branding and marketing begin to inform sales and commerce in real time. Sales and commerce communicate demand signals directly into operations and fulfillment. Operations and fulfillment provide immediate performance feedback into customer engagement and service delivery. Finance and accounting no longer merely report what happened after the fact, but help shape decisions with timely insight grounded in live enterprise data. The business starts to behave less like a collection of separate functions and more like an integrated system.

This shift is essential because the next generation of enterprise performance depends on three capabilities that cannot fully mature inside silos: Hyper-automation, Hyper-personalization and Data-driven decision making.

Hyper-automation cannot thrive where processes break at functional handoffs. If a customer-facing workflow begins in marketing, moves into sales, triggers fulfillment, generates service needs, and ends in finance, then automating only one step in one department creates limited value. True Hyper-automation requires horizontally connected processes, common data structures, interoperable systems, and shared operational logic across the enterprise. The more horizontally integrated the business becomes, the more automation can move from isolated task automation to end-to-end business orchestration.

The same is true of Hyper-personalization. Personalization is often misunderstood as a marketing capability alone. It is not. True personalization is enterprise-wide. It is the ability to shape experiences, products, services, communications, pricing, fulfillment models and ongoing support based on an integrated understanding of the customer, the context and the moment. To operate in this manner requires data to travel horizontally across functions. A company cannot be truly personalized if marketing knows one version of the customer, sales knows another, service knows a third, and finance knows only transactional history. Hyper-personalization emerges when the enterprise acts from a unified understanding rather than fragmented observations.

Data-driven decision making also depends on horizontal integration. Data trapped inside vertical systems becomes departmental reporting. Data integrated horizontally becomes enterprise intelligence. The difference is enormous. Departmental reporting helps leaders explain yesterday. Enterprise intelligence helps leaders shape tomorrow. When Digital Enablement removes the structural barriers between systems, teams and business units, data can begin to inform decisions at the speed required by the modern economy. This is especially critical for global enterprises, where complexity is multiplied by geography, product lines, channels, regulatory environments and regional operating models. Without horizontal digital integration, global scale becomes a drag on responsiveness. With it, global scale becomes an advantage.

This is why the Automated Economy demands a new paradigm. It is not enough to digitize isolated functions. It is not enough to modernize systems one department at a time. It is not enough to install better tools into old silos and expect enterprise acceleration to occur. The enterprise must be rethought as a connected digital organism—one in which technology is not a vertical support function, but a horizontal operating reality woven into the full fabric of the business.

That shift is not cosmetic. It changes leadership responsibility. It changes operating design. It changes investment priorities. It changes how organizations define accountability, how they structure teams, how they govern data, how they design workflows, and how they measure performance. It requires leaders to stop asking, "What system does this department need?" and begin asking, "How should this capability operate across the enterprise?" This is a far more strategic question and it is the right one we need to be asking.

The companies that embrace this horizontal model will move faster. They will see across the enterprise more clearly. They will reduce friction between business units. They will create stronger continuity from demand creation to demand fulfillment to customer retention. They will unlock automation at scale, personalization with precision and decision-making with speed and confidence. Most importantly, they will be positioned to grow revenue more intentionally, improve operational efficiency more materially and use data not merely as a reporting asset, but as a strategic force multiplier.

As Albert Einstein warned, we cannot solve today's problems with the same level of thinking that created them. We must think anew. And the remainder of this book is about how to do exactly that—clearly, deliberately, and fast enough to matter.

QUICK ASSESSMENT

We invite you to take a moment and consider your situation, your company, your enterprise.

Where is your organization's digital maturity today? How can you know?

Take a moment and complete this quick assessment:

The buyer decides what is valuable, what scales, and what survives.

PART ONE

MACRO DISRUPTIONS

"Times are changing." This is the phrase people reach for when acceleration becomes undeniable. It appears most often in challenging, uncertain, and compressed periods. Results take more effort. Customer expectations shift mid-cycle. Strategies decay faster than they can be deployed. The phrase is common because the feeling of being left behind is common. But that feeling is not the explanation.

In business, when the feelings are stripped away, "times are changing" means something more specific. Buyer behavior continues to accelerate. Business models accelerate in response. Learning models are rewritten to keep up. Businesses are being created to disrupt the status quo. Innovation compounds and delivers greater value in the client experience. **From inside the**

moment, it feels like times are changing. They are. And when you are in it, you often cannot even see it.

Macro disruptions explain why.

UNDERSTANDING MACRO DISRUPTIONS

Looking back across history, we have seen that change, when it occurred at all, moved slowly, with long periods of backsliding. Tools improved incrementally. The shape of a plow might change, and the animal pulling it might change, but it was still muscle pulling a plow. Big advances did occur, such as domestication and farming, but they were rare. The stone age evolved into the copper age, then the bronze age, then the iron age. The time between each age was measured in centuries. The industrial age did not begin until around 1760, roughly 3,000 years after the beginning of the iron age.

The same pattern applies in modes of commerce. Grain and livestock were standards in the means of exchange for centuries. Eventually coins made of silver, copper, or gold became standard. In the early 11th century, a copper shortage caused the Song dynasty in China to issue the first paper currency. Some 1,100 years later, money is now largely electrons. It can be stored on a small piece of plastic, a credit card, which has existed for roughly 70 years since its introduction in 1958. Money can also be stored on your smartphone, a device that has been common for roughly 18 years, with an e-wallet that has existed for roughly 13 years.

The 21st-century economy moves at electron speed, the speed of light. It took nearly half a century for 50 percent of households to own a car. Smartphone usage took roughly five years to reach 50 percent. Artificial intelligence has been widely available for only a few years. Yet AI, as it is referred to, is already everywhere. It is in medicine, architecture, manufacturing, retail, and on your phone. The speed of change is now so fast that it is increasingly difficult to keep up without the help of the same technologies accelerating the change. New discoveries, new products, new services, and new business models appear and disappear at a rate that feels almost continuous. This is not randomness. It is macro disruption.

Macro disruptions are eternal. They have been driven by the buyer, whether business or individual, since the beginning of commerce. The ability to recognize the buyer mindset that has continuously driven these disruptions is essential to removing fear and embracing the adoption of Digital Enablement across the enterprise. The enterprise can be five people with ten products or services, or ten thousand people delivering hundreds of products and services. The operating condition is the same.

Macro disruptions are cyclical transformations that continuously reshape the structure of global economies, industries, and societies.

These disruptions emerge from the interaction of three enduring forces:

- The rapid expansion of choices
- Evolving business models
- Evolving learning models

Each cycle is amplified by the buyer's obsession to obtain what they want, when they want it, and at the value they want it. Across every era, from agricultural to industrial, from computer to digital, these forces interact to form a continuous disruption cycle. It repeatedly redefines production, distribution, and commerce.

As with every macro disruption, some players evolve by creating. Some evolve by embracing. Some miss emerging technologies. Some ultimately become extinct.

The driver underneath the cycle is not technology. Technology is the amplifier. The driver is the buyer.

Buyer behavior drives change. Innovation drives the expansion of change. Innovators create new options and a resulting expansion of choices. These new options are viewed as valuable by some class of buyers. As early adopters expand the market, implementers enter to increase supply. Prices drop and the market expands. As expansion occurs, pressure increases on competitive business models.

Amazon illustrates how this compounds. In the beginning there were local bookshops, even libraries for obtaining and reading books. Then came bookstore chains like Barnes & Noble and Borders. Then came the internet and Amazon. Amazon offered a long tail of books, meaning a vast catalog of niche and low-volume titles that physical stores could not efficiently stock. It offered them at low prices and could get them in the buyer's hands in two or three days. Probably more than any other company, Amazon helped accelerate the buyer mindset that is the norm: "I want what I want, when I want it, at the value I want it." Amazon also pioneered the recommendation engine, allowing it to recommend products that prior purchases indicated a buyer would likely want. Amazon even patented one-click purchase, a simple consumer feature but a high-value micro-disruption for businesses. Think about it: how often do you default to Amazon without even considering alternatives, and what does that reveal about the expectations you now carry into every buying experience?

Macro disruption does not occur only in consumer categories. Business-to-business products and services are part of a giant ecosystem that ultimately produces a product or service for an end buyer. The iPhone supply chain alone encompasses thousands of companies with millions of total employees across many countries. The F-35 Lightning fighter jet's final buyer is the U.S. Air Force and other air forces throughout the world. To build it requires large networks of suppliers across states and nations. These are classified as B2B, but they all contribute to building a product purchased by a buyer. In macro disruption, there is no separation. There is only the buyer's standard and the systems built to meet it.

THE THREE FORCES OF MACRO DISRUPTIONS

1. The Rapid Expansion of Choices

The first force of macro disruption is the rapid expansion of choices.

The rapid expansion of choices represents the widening spectrum of products, services, and experiences available to both retail buyers and enterprises. Every technological leap, business model innovation, or social shift multiplies available options. Competition intensifies. Expectations reset.

Over time, each wave of Digital Enablement, from the Agrarian Era through the Digital Era, has democratized access and compressed decision cycles. This expansion creates abundance, but it also imposes cognitive and operational complexity.

The expansion of choices manifests across the three timeless dimensions of buyer behavior.

- What we want becomes commoditized across categories such as packaged goods, automotive, and housing.
- When we want it shifts toward same-day and instant expectations across industries including household goods, groceries, pharmaceuticals, and even housing.
- At the value we want it produces extreme stratification, from near-zero fast fashion to luxury delivered through mass-market platforms.

Choice expansion is not a side effect. It is the initiating force. It is the primary signal that a market is destabilizing. From an executive perspective, choice expansion is the earliest and most reliable indicator that equilibrium is breaking. Long before business models break, operating margins compress, or workforce skills fall behind, leaders see something more immediate. Customers suddenly have more alternatives than ever before.

Comparison becomes instantaneous. What once required time, effort, or physical presence now occurs in seconds. Choice expands first. Everything else reacts.

This is why rapid expansion of choices must be treated as the first force of macro disruption. It is the force that removes equilibrium from markets and sets in motion the need for new business models and new learning models. Organizations that misinterpret this as noise, competition, or temporary volatility respond too late.

Macro disruption does not begin with technology. It begins when buyers realize they have rapidly expanding choices and options.

Customers suddenly have more alternatives than ever before.

Choice expansion compounds across economic eras. It does not replace the prior era. It builds upon it. Each era inherits the production, distribution and commerce capabilities of the one before it, then extends them through new forms of enablement.

In the Agrarian Era, choice was local, seasonal, and limited. Production dictated availability, distribution was manual and commerce required proximity.

In the Industrial Era, mechanization, standardization and scale expanded availability and expanded geographic reach. Goods could be produced in far greater volume, transported more broadly and sold more consistently across markets. Brands emerged to distinguish similar products, and buyers began to encounter more options than any prior era had made possible. Even so, decision cycles remained relatively slow, information remained unevenly distributed, and most choices were still shaped more by producer capacity than by real-time buyer preference.

In the Computerized Era, enterprises began to digitize information, formalize processes, and manage complexity at scale. Computing systems improved planning, inventory control, financial management, procurement and operational coordination across larger and more distributed organizations. Choice expanded not merely because more products could be made, but because businesses could now organize, categorize, forecast and replenish with greater precision. Retailers and manufacturers gained the ability to manage broader assortments, support more SKUs and reduce stockouts and coordinate supply across expanding channels. Buyers still did not possess instant transparency, but organizations became far more capable of presenting structured choice, segmenting offerings and serving diverse market needs with greater consistency.

In the Digital Era, information asymmetry collapsed. Comparison became immediate. Reviews, pricing, specifications, substitutes and alternatives were exposed in real time. The marginal cost of presenting another option approached zero. Platforms began to anticipate needs, personalize offerings, dynamically price products, and continuously re-bundle services. Search itself started to change. In many cases, the buyer no longer initiates discovery in the traditional sense; choices arrive pre-curated, context-aware and increasingly optimized around behavior, intent and predicted demand.

For example, on platforms such as Amazon, buyers are increasingly presented with recommended products, bundled offers, and replenishment prompts before conducting a traditional search. Likewise, on platforms such as Netflix or Spotify, users are often guided by algorithmically curated recommendations rather than initiating discovery from a blank starting point. In both cases, choice is no longer merely searched for; it is increasingly surfaced, sequenced, and optimized in advance. Executives are not managing a single era of choice expansion. They are operating within stacked eras simultaneously. Failure to recognize this produces misdiagnosis of market behavior and flawed strategic responses.

Considering how impactful the rapid expansion of choices is, which creates an abundance of opportunity, it also introduces destabilization. Two forces appear immediately: cognitive overload and operational complexity. As options proliferate, buyers simplify decisions through shortcuts, defaults, brand proxies, or platforms that decide on their behalf. This is not a failure of intelligence. It is a rational response to abundance. **Customers are not empowered by infinite choice. They are exhausted by it.**

That exhaustion creates opportunity for intermediaries to emerge. Platforms, aggregators, and ecosystems gain power not by offering more choice, but by reducing the effort required to choose. They succeed by simplifying decision-making in an environment of overwhelming optionality.

Enterprises experience the same complexity internally. Product sprawl increases. Processes fragment. Decision cycles slow.

Organizations built for scarcity struggle to function effectively in abundance.

Digital platforms do not merely host choice. They manufacture it.

By separating production, distribution and commerce, platforms allow thousands of suppliers to coexist, compete, and evolve simultaneously. The result is exponential growth in available options without corresponding growth in buyer effort.

This is where the executive strategic question shifts. The question is no longer only, "What do we sell?" It becomes, "How do buyers find, compare, and decide?" Power shifts away from producers and toward orchestrators of ecosystems. The organization that controls discovery and decision flow captures disproportionate value, regardless of who produces the underlying goods or services.

Most legacy enterprises were designed for scarcity, not abundance. They assume stable portfolios, predictable demand, linear customer journeys, and slow feedback cycles. Choice expansion invalidates those assumptions simultaneously. The consequences appear quickly. Portfolios expand without clarity. Marketing messages proliferate without differentiation. Supply chains optimize for outdated patterns. Leadership teams struggle to decide faster than markets move.

Organizations do not lose because competitors are better. They lose because they cannot metabolize choice fast enough.

In an environment defined by abundance, **executive responsibility shifts from managing offerings to architecting decision environments.** This requires intentional constraint, not unlimited expansion. Fewer internal choices, clearer priorities and a digitally enabled enterprise that reduces friction becomes a strategic advantage. Digital Enablement through Hyper-automation, Hyper-personalization and Data-driven decision making must serve clarity. When they do not, they amplify noise. The organizations that survive macro disruption do not attempt to offer everything. They become exceptional at helping buyers decide.

The rapid expansion of choices is the initiating force that triggers the other macro disruption elements.

2. Evolving Business Models

The second force is evolving business models.

Evolving business models are a direct result of the rapid expansion of choices. As choice expands, business models adapt to accommodate abundance. Some expose blind spots. Others exploit opportunity. Models that successfully take advantage of expanding choices across all three buyer dimensions must be purposefully designed.

Digital Enablement allows leaders to shift their thinking by understanding the impact and outcomes of these new business models rather than being constrained by legacy assumptions. As the availability of choices continues to multiply, business models must continuously adapt.

Evolving business models are not the result of creativity alone. They are the inevitable consequence of macro disruptions, and most critically, of the rapid expansion of choices available to buyers.

As choice expands, power migrates away from producers and towards buyers. When buyers gain alternatives, transparency, speed, and flexibility, legacy business models begin to fracture. Some fracture slowly, appearing stable until margins erode. Others fail abruptly when a competitor reframes value entirely.

The executive mistake is to treat business model evolution as:

- A marketing exercise
- A pricing strategy
- A technology upgrade

In reality, business model evolution is a structural response to buyer power.

A business model defines:

- How value is created
- How value is delivered
- How value is monetized
- How risk is allocated

Macro disruptions force each of these elements to change simultaneously.

As we consider the buyer obsession for "what we want, when we want it, at the value we want it," macro disruption changes the buyer's tolerance for compromise. Historically, buyers accepted limited availability, slow fulfilment, opaque pricing, and blinded inefficiencies. By 'blinded inefficiencies,' we mean the hidden frictions buyers once had little power to detect or challenge: uncertain inventory, delayed fulfillment, inconsistent pricing, disconnected service experiences, manual approval bottlenecks, poor logistics visibility, and slow issue resolution. These inefficiencies long existed inside the enterprise, but digital transparency exposed them to the market. As digital infrastructure, logistics networks, and data intelligence matured, those compromises became unnecessary, and eventually, unacceptable.

Business models that fail today are not defeated by competitors; they are rejected by buyers.

This distinction matters. Competition implies rivalry. Rejection implies irrelevance.

In any era, this business model evolution is happening, and currently we are moving from goods centric models to outcome centric models. Traditional industrial capitalism was built on a simple exchange—manufacture a product, sell ownership of such product, recognize revenue at point of sale. This traditional model assumes the buyer wants ownership, the buyer can manage the asset, the buyer bears operational risk, and value ends at delivery. These assumptions are no longer universally valid. Ownership is increasingly seen as friction, not value.

We are currently experiencing a shift toward services that include a "thing." Consider how this has already played out in everyday life.

Spotify does not sell music files. It sells access to any song, instantly.

Netflix does not sell DVDs. It sells on-demand entertainment.

Uber does not sell cars. It sells transportation on demand.

Another example is through cars and insurance.

Traditionally, a customer buys a car and separately purchases insurance. They manage maintenance, depreciation, and risk.

In an outcome-based model, the customer does not buy a car—they purchase mobility. One provider delivers the vehicle, insurance, maintenance, and upgrades as a bundled service. The customer pays for access and reliability, not ownership. The "thing" (the car) still exists, but it is embedded within the service.

Modern business models increasingly invert the relationship. The buyer wants the outcome. The provider manages the complexity, and the asset becomes a means, not a product.

In this modern model, the "thing" is embedded within the service. Revenue shifts from transactional to recurring while risk shifts from buyer to provider, enabling value to be measured continuously, not simply one time.

This is not semantic; it is structural.

Further, in evolving models, manufacturing does not disappear; it is repositioned. The purpose of manufacturing now shifts from producing units for resale, to producing assets that enable a service promise.

A manufacturer building for resale optimizes unit cost, throughput, and inventory turns. A manufacturer building for service optimization prioritizes reliability over lifespan, predictive maintenance, upgradeability, and total cost of ownership. These are fundamentally different design philosophies that require different cost structures, different quality thresholds, different lifecycle assumptions, and significantly different data instrumentation.

For executives, this shift introduces tension. Revenue recognition moves from upfront to recurring. Capital intensity may increase. Cash flow timing changes. New asset depreciation strategies evolve.

In this macro shift, the upside is quite material. There are higher lifetime values, lower churn, pricing variance through differentiation and significantly defensible moats through operational complexity.

The executive question is no longer "Is this risky?" It is now "What risk are we already carrying by not changing?"

Consider the evolution of physical mail delivery. Over centuries, delivery models progressed from the Pony Express to the railroad and eventually to the traditional postal service. These models evolved naturally with infrastructure improvements.

Then an innovator, FedEx, embraced buyer obsession and reimagined the promise of delivery. They considered a longstanding model, once centered on a single stamp costing only a few cents, and created next-day delivery. "When it absolutely, positively has to be there overnight." Immediately an entirely new business model was born. This was not incremental improvement. It was a structural redefinition of speed, value, and reliability. This was not faster mail. This was certainty as a product. FedEx did not sell delivery. FedEx sold time compression and risk elimination. The envelope was incidental.

Consider the reasons for this macro disruption. FedEx rebuilt logistics around time guarantees. They designed infrastructure for reliability, not cost. They monetized urgency, not postage and they shifted buyer expectations permanently. Once buyers experienced overnight certainty, all other models were doomed. This is the hallmark for business model evolution. The new business model makes previous tradeoffs obsolete. It resets the buyer's baseline. It forces industry-wide reconfiguration.

Modern markets normalize models such as subscription, freemium, e-commerce, advertising, marketplace, and direct-to-consumer. Each is a response to buyer behavior and expanding choice. Each becomes dominant for a period and is then pressured by the next wave of enablement.

Even so, headline labels are not the full model. Terms such as subscription, marketplace, direct-to-consumer, or services-based describe the business at a surface level, but they do not explain the full operating architecture underneath. A deeper model captures how the enterprise actually creates value, delivers it, monetizes it, and sustains it over time.

Southwest Airlines is a useful example. When it began in the 1970s, Southwest relied on low fares, quick turnarounds for on-time flights and distinctive customer service. It kept prices low by avoiding major airports and operating from less convenient airports. Its point-to-point network reduced nonstop options. It flew only one type of plane, reducing training complexity. Its model was coherent with its promise.

Its competitor, American Airlines, pursued a different buyer. It offered frequent flights to primary airports and broad destinations, with higher-priced tickets aimed at the business traveler. Different buyer, different promise, different system.

Neither model remained intact. Southwest still sells tickets at a lower price point than American, but open seating is no longer what it was. It flies to major airports. Its service posture has faded. It has layoffs like any other airline. American was unable to avoid bankruptcy and has trimmed destinations, reduced flights, increased prices, and seen service decline. The point is not which airline won. The point is that changing times eventually render all business models obsolete.

Until just before the turn of the century, e-commerce and freemium models did not exist. They were innovations born with the internet. Subscription models existed primarily for print publications and books. Even as technology-driven change increased in speed and impact, new business models initially evolved slowly to meet new customer demands. Many companies dismissed the internet as a fad and failed to build models that incorporated it. Others assumed its impact would occur far faster than it did. Brick-and-mortar retailers did not vanish overnight, but footprints contracted and pressure intensified. One

The point is that changing times eventually render all business models obsolete.

after another, innovations keep coming and consumer demand keeps changing. Businesses that adapt quickly succeed. Those that do not risk becoming obsolete.

In these cases, Digital Enablement is the catalyst, not the strategy. Digital Enablement does not create the new business model by itself. It does something more subtle, and more dangerous to incumbents. It removes the constraints that justified the old ones.

Utilizing Digital Enablement provides the catalyst for acceleration. Digital systems enable real time data feedback, predictive intelligence, continuous pricing modifications and dynamic fulfillment orchestration.

These capabilities allow leaders to design models around outcomes, not transactions.

There is a pattern in business model failures. Trying to digitize an already broken model, automating inefficiency and seeking to accelerate irrelevance. These can be avoided by simply taking steps to gain much needed clarity for where they currently exist. An obvious area once clarity is obtained is recognizing Digital Enablement must be strategically paired with effective process redesign.

Simultaneously, there are patterns for evolving effective business models. These have been seen across various industries, where recurring patterns are emerging through macro disruptions. One example is Product as a Service (PaaS).

Consider Rolls-Royce in its jet engine business. Airlines do not simply purchase engines outright. Instead, Rolls-Royce offers a "Power by the Hour" model, where airlines pay based on engine usage. Rolls-Royce monitors engine performance in real time, performs maintenance proactively, and guarantees uptime. The airline is not buying an engine. It is buying reliable thrust and operational certainty.

In this case, equipment bundled with uptime guarantees, maintenance imbedded within a subscription, and performance being measured throughout the product lifecycle.

Another example is Outcome-Based pricing, in which the enterprise is paid for usage, availability, performance or achieved results rather than simply for product delivery. For example, in digital advertising, companies pay for clicks or conversions rather than the ad itself. In manufacturing, providers may be paid based on equipment uptime or output produced. In healthcare, some treatments are now priced based on patient outcomes.

These emerging models are far from trends. They represent a massive disruption to traditional models many have become accustomed to and are being created to the response of the buyer leverage resulting from the rapid expansion of choices within various industries.

The awareness for business models evolving often reveal blind spots for us as executives. The very fact that *Blind Spots* exist allows for many executives to hinder and often stop the very progress toward new models being innovated within our own enterprises. Executives often experience failure for evolving business models through the very existence of legacy margins, trying to optimize what has been for a few more periods. We often seek to protect revenue streams, instead of paying attention to our client relationships that have proven successful over time. Additionally, we may try and treat services as add-ons instead of realizing the very service may be at the core for evolving to new business models.

One of the most dangerous phrases often used and heard in executive discussions is "That's not how our industry works!" Macro disruptions do not care about industry boundaries.

Evolving business models are not a one-time transaction or event, or even a one-time transformation.

To effectively evolve business models requires four primary areas for focus. These are:

- Continuous sensing/connecting with buyer behavior
- Modular operating models
- Flexible pricing architectures
- Technology that enables change, versus technology that "locks it out"

Further, for executives, the strategic objective is not perfection. The objective is adaptability at speed!

We all are aware change is constant, and we have all lived through enough of it to confirm this reality. As we look ahead in the evolving business models, our view for defining the winners for the next decade, will not come from the best manufacturers, the fastest adopters of technology or the lowest cost producers. **The enterprises that will win will be the ones able to redesign themselves around buyer outcomes, treat producers as enablers, not endpoints, and monetize certainty, reliability and time**.

Manufacturing (production) will not disappear. It will evolve from manufacturing (production) for resale and increasingly give way to manufacturing for service enablement. This is not an evolution of pricing. This is an evolution of purpose.

3. Evolving Learning Models

Learning models eventually adjust.

The third force of macro disruption is not technological in isolation, nor is it economic in the traditional sense. It is epistemological; the speed at which learning will occur will be phenomenal, cognitive acceleration will be the norm. How knowledge is created, transferred, validated, and operationalized inside modern enterprises will be utterly transformed.

For over a century, learning has been treated as something that happens *before* work begins. Formal education systems, particularly K-12 and universities, were designed to front-load knowledge under the assumption that the world learners would enter was relatively stable. This assumption has collapsed.

Digital Enablement has compressed the half-life of skills to such a degree that knowledge acquisition detached from execution has become strategically insufficient. The rate at which business models evolve now exceeds the rate at which traditional institutions can update curricula, accredit programs, or graduate talent.

Educators have not failed in this regard. It is a structural mismatch between learning velocity and business velocity—the rate at which an enterprise acquires, applies and operationalizes new knowledge.

The result is a macro disruption: learning itself is evolving from a static, institution-centric model into a **dynamic, embedded, enterprise-driven capability**.

We are consistently experiencing a mismatch between legacy education and digital business velocity. Legacy education models were engineered for a world where:

- Knowledge changed slowly
- Careers followed linear progression
- Authority flowed top-down

- Experience accumulated over decades
- Mastery preceded responsibility

None of these assumptions remain valid.

Digital businesses operate in environments where:

- Tools change quarterly
- Business models pivot annually
- Competitive advantages erode rapidly
- Organizational boundaries blur
- Value is created at the edge, not the center

Universities still optimize for content coverage, while enterprises require capability acquisition. Schools assess retention, while businesses demand application. Degrees certify completion, but companies need continuous competence.

The consequence is not merely inefficiency. It is risk.

Executives increasingly discover that hiring "qualified" talent does not equate to operational readiness. New employees arrive credentialed yet underprepared for the real systems, data flows, decision rights, and digital tools that define modern enterprises.

This gap is widening, not narrowing.

We are rapidly moving from credential-based learning to capability-based learning. The emerging learning model does not begin with degrees. It begins with outcomes.

In a digitally enabled enterprise, learning is re-anchored to four operational realities:

- What outcomes must this role produce?
- What systems does this role touch?

- What decisions does this role influence?
- What knowledge decays fastest in this role?

This reframing shifts learning from credential-based legitimacy to capability-based relevance.

The most advanced organizations no longer ask:

"Where did you learn this?"

They ask:

"How fast can you learn what changes next?"

This distinction is subtle but profound. It replaces pedigree with adaptability and replaces static expertise with learning velocity as a core performance metric. An actual learning by doing is the current reality in business and quickly becoming the dominant model.

One of the clearest signals of evolving learning models is the rise of learning-by-doing pathways. Programs such as alternative fellowships, self-directed coding communities, creator economies, and hands-on digital apprenticeships have demonstrated something legacy institutions struggle to accept: Competence emerges faster when learning is inseparable from execution.

When individuals learn while producing real outcomes, several accelerants appear simultaneously:

- Immediate feedback loops
- Contextual relevance
- Emotional engagement

- Economic incentive
- Rapid iteration

This is why digital natives often outperform traditionally trained peers in fast-moving environments. They are not necessarily more intelligent; they are more conditioned to learn in motion.

Organizations that fail to internalize this reality will continue to experience friction between "training" and "performance."

So what does one do? The best enterprises have become the new learning institutions, as a critical inversion is underway: Businesses are becoming the primary educators of their workforce.

This does not mean companies will replace universities. It means they can no longer depend on them as the primary source of job-ready capability.

Modern enterprises are beginning to design learning infrastructure as deliberately as they design supply chains or financial systems. Learning platforms, digital playbooks, embedded simulations, AI-driven coaching, and role-specific knowledge graphs are becoming core enterprise assets.

The most mature organizations recognize that:

- Onboarding is not orientation; it is acceleration.
- Training is not episodic; it is continuous.
- Knowledge is not centralized; it is contextual.
- Learning is not uniform; it is adaptive.

This marks a fundamental shift from education as a phase to learning as an operating system where real time learning is taking place at the point of work. In evolving learning models, the most valuable learning occurs at the moment of decision.

Static courses, long seminars, and generic certifications are increasingly ineffective because they separate knowledge acquisition from the cognitive context in which it is applied.

By contrast, real-time learning systems:

- Surface guidance inside workflows
- Adapt content based on role, behavior, and performance
- Reinforce learning through repetition in context
- Shorten time-to-competence dramatically

This is the difference between *knowing* and *performing*.

Executives should view this not as an HR initiative, but as a throughput optimization problem. Faster learning directly correlates to faster execution, lower error rates, and higher organizational agility.

There are real differences between adaptive learning and individual cognitive styles.

One of the most underappreciated failures of traditional education is its insistence on uniformity. Everyone receives the same content, in the same format, at the same pace.

Digital learning systems shatter this constraint.

Adaptive learning recognizes that employees differ across multiple dimensions:

- Prior knowledge
- Cognitive processing speed

- Preferred learning modality
- Risk tolerance
- Decision confidence

Modern learning architectures can now adjust dynamically, modifying depth, pacing, and reinforcement based on observed behavior rather than assumed averages.

From an executive perspective, this is not a "soft" benefit. It is a capital efficiency gain.

Faster learners are no longer constrained by slower cohorts, and slower learners are no longer left behind.

Perhaps we are finally experiencing the collapse of military-influenced leadership models.

The evolution of learning models cannot be separated from the evolution of leadership models.

Most corporate hierarchies were inherited from military and industrial structures optimized for command-and-control, predictability, and compliance. These systems assumed that knowledge flowed downward and execution flowed upward.

Digital Enterprises invert this flow.

Today, insight often originates at the edge of the organization—from developers, analysts, operators, and creators who interact directly with systems and data. Leadership increasingly depends on sense-making, not instruction.

Learning models that reinforce rigid hierarchy now actively suppress value creation.

Executives must confront an uncomfortable truth: Many leadership frameworks taught over the last century have aged one hundred years in just the past five.

Think about static knowledge in a dynamic world. Think encyclopedias. Think textbooks.

These artifacts were optimized for preservation, not adaptation. Digital Enablement renders them insufficient as primary learning vehicles.

Knowledge today must be:

- Continuously updated
- Easily searchable
- Contextually delivered
- Rapidly deprecated

Organizations that continue to treat knowledge as a static asset will experience increasing organizational drag. Those that treat learning as a living system will out-learn competitors regardless of size or capital.

For CEOs, CFOs, and various other leaders, there are significant strategic implications.

Learning velocity is now a competitive advantage. Strategy execution depends less on long-term plans and more on the organization's ability to absorb change.

Embedded learning reduces waste, lowers attrition, and accelerates time-to-productivity. Learning infrastructure should be evaluated as a return-generating asset, not an overhead cost.

Operational excellence increasingly depends on workforce adaptability. Learning systems must be integrated into process design, not layered on top of it.

The most successful enterprises of the next decade will not be those with the best products, the largest balance sheets, or the most recognized brands. They will be those that learn faster than the environments they operate in.

Evolving learning models are not a Human Resources trend. They are a macro disruption reshaping how value is created, sustained, and scaled. Organizations that fail to internalize this shift will continue hiring for yesterday, training for last year, and competing in markets that no longer exist. Those that embrace it will build enterprises that evolve as quickly as the world around

Faster learners are no longer constrained by slower cohorts, and slower learners are no longer left behind.

them.

In a quick summary, **macro disruption is the convergence of expanding choices, evolving business models, and accelerated learning systems**.

As executives, we invite you to consider this: disruption cannot be resisted. It must be harnessed through intentional strategy, leadership, and Digital Enablement.

Macro disruptions are cyclical transformations that continuously reshape the structure of global economies, industries, and societies.

PART TWO

THE AUTOMATED ECONOMY

THE ECONOMY WAS ALWAYS MOVING HERE

Every era arrives quietly before it is recognized loudly. It does not announce itself with a single invention or a singular event. It forms as choices multiply; business models stretch beyond their original intent and learning cycles regenerate fast enough to create a new normal. What defines an era is not novelty—it is inevitability. When buyer behavior changes faster than institutions can respond, the conditions for a new era are already in place.

The Automated Economy is not a distant future state. It is already present structurally in our current reality, even though operational adoption remains uneven across industries, companies and geographies. The Automated Economy is the natural continuation of an ancient human pattern.

As we mentioned in the previous chapter, history confirms this pattern. The agrarian era gave way to industrialization not because farms failed, but because scale, speed, and consistency became decisive advantages. The industrial era yielded to computing as information overtook machinery as the primary driver of productivity. Each transition followed the same arc: expanding choice, evolving business models, and new learning systems that compressed time and increased expectations. Once enough participants adopted the new model, the previous era did not disappear—it became insufficient.

We are living through such a transition now.

From the earliest recorded trade between villages to today's algorithmic marketplaces, the economy has always been driven by a single immutable force: **the buyer's desire to get what they want, when they want it, at the value they believe it is worth**. Every economic era, system, and innovation is merely a response to that demand.

What distinguishes the Automated Economy from prior eras is not intent, but **velocity, scale, and precision**. For the first time in history, economic systems are capable of responding to buyer demand in **near real time**, across global markets, with continuously adapting structures. Automation is no longer confined to machines or software. It now includes **business models, organizational design, decision-making, and value delivery** itself.

An era forms when innovation regenerates faster than organizations can absorb it. As businesses compete to meet rising buyer expectations, they introduce new promises into the market—faster delivery, greater personalization, lower friction, higher perceived value. Early innovators experiment. Implementers follow. Standards emerge. What was once extraordinary becomes expected. Efficiency then sets in.

Efficiency is the quiet inflection point. It lowers cost, increases comfort, and creates predictability. And with predictability comes complacency. The very systems that once powered growth begin to resist change. Fear replaces curiosity. Optimization replaces imagination. This is when opportunity opens—not for incremental improvement, but for reinvention.

What distinguishes the Automated Economy from prior eras is not intent, but velocity, scale, and precision.

Then, someone chooses to innovate again.

As that innovation scales, micro disruptions ripple across the market. New entrants bypass legacy constraints. Business models fracture and reform. Learning cycles accelerate. Eventually, the accumulation of these micro disruptions crosses a threshold—and a new era emerges.

This is not a failure of leadership or effort. It is a structural reality. Every era ends because it succeeds too well at solving yesterday's problems.

This is a moment in considering a shift of legacy thinking to reframe how you have thought of automation. Automation is not a technological trend, but the structural maturation of the economy.

THE BUYER AS THE PRIME MOVER OF ALL ECONOMIES

Every economy begins and ends with the buyer. This statement appears obvious, yet it is frequently ignored in enterprise strategy. Organizations often design around products, factories, supply chains, or internal efficiency metrics. Economies, however, do not move because things are produced. They move because **buyers choose**.

Economies move because buyers choose.

While technologies change, one principle persists across every era: the ability to scale consistently determines who thrives. Hyper-scaling organizations are not simply bigger; they are faster, more connected, and more responsive to the buyer.

Success has always belonged to those who deliver on the buyer promise—what the buyer wants, when they want it, at the value they are willing to pay. As buyer audiences expand, business models must evolve to serve them. As volume increases,

Economies move because buyers choose.

efficiency becomes non-negotiable. And efficiency, at scale, is always powered by automation.

Automation is not about replacing people. It is about eliminating friction. It is the mechanism by which promises are delivered repeatedly, reliably, and profitably. In every era, automation sits at the center of scale. What changes is where automation lives and how quickly it must adapt.

The Automated Economy represents the most advanced expression of buyer-centricity in human history. It removes friction between desire and fulfillment. It compresses time between intent and acquisition. It reduces waste between value created and value realized.

The Timeless Buyer Obsession

Across all eras, the buyer's obsession has remained constant:

1. What do I want?
2. When do I want it?
3. What am I willing to exchange for it?

Agrarian societies answered this obsession locally and seasonally. Industrial economies answered it at scale but slowly. Digital economies answer it continuously, globally and dynamically.

The Automated Economy answers it **predictively**.

In this sense, automation is about **aligning economic systems more precisely with human desire**. The buyer obsession prevails and continues to accelerate. Being able to deliver on the buyer promise is a requirement to sustainability and the Automated Economy ensures it.

Today's economy is no longer defined by computing power alone. We have moved beyond an era where technology simply supports the business. We are now in an era where technology *is* the business model.

This shift has been driven by an onslaught of micro disruptions:

- Cloud-based platforms replacing fixed infrastructure
- Subscription and usage-based models displacing ownership
- Real-time data replacing retrospective reporting
- Artificial intelligence augmenting decision-making
- Automation collapsing time across marketing, sales, operations and service

Individually, none of these disruptions are decisive. Collectively, they are transformational.

Entire industries are being reshaped—not incrementally improved, but overtaken. Retailers built on physical footprints are displaced by digitally native platforms. Transportation models are redefined by software rather than fleets. Hospitality scales without owning property. Financial services fragment into embedded experiences.

These are not technology stories. They are buyer stories.

Buyers now expect immediacy, relevance, and value as a baseline. Organizations that cannot respond at that speed are not competing—they are waiting to be replaced.

The Automated Economy is the fulfillment of the buyer promise through digitally enabled models that expand choice, compress time and scale value delivery automatically.

In this economy, growth is no longer driven by adding people, layers, or complexity. It is driven by alignment—of people, processes, systems, and data—designed to operate at the speed of buyer behavior.

Automation becomes the connective tissue that links intent to execution. Data replaces assumption. Decisions move closer to real time. Personalization scales without manual intervention. Learning loops tighten continuously.

Organizations either participate in this economy—or they are automated by it.

THE CORE SYSTEMS OF THE AUTOMATED ECONOMY

Across history, business models evolve in three consistent dimensions:

1. **Production**—How value is created
2. **Distribution**—How value reaches the buyer
3. **Commerce**—How value is consumed

In the Automated Economy, all three dimensions are transforming simultaneously. Production is increasingly standardized and modularized, enabling faster iteration and global reach. Distribution is instantaneous and omnichannel by default. Commerce is fluid, recurring and usage driven. Options are no longer limited by shelf space or geography—they expand continuously.

As production becomes easier and distribution faster, competition shifts away from who can build and toward who can *enable*. The advantage belongs to those who can sense buyer behavior, respond dynamically and deliver consistently at scale.

These systems exist in every economy, regardless of era or technology. What changes over time is **how they are structured, coordinated, and optimized**.

Means of Production

The means of production encompass how value is created. This includes:

- Labor models
- Capital deployment
- Manufacturing and service creation
- Knowledge and intellectual property
- Automation of creation itself

In the Automated Economy, production is no longer optimized solely for efficiency or scale. It is optimized for **responsiveness and configurability**. Production systems increasingly adapt to demand signals rather than forecast averages.

Mass production gives way to **mass configuration**.

Means of Distribution

Distribution determines how value moves from producer to buyer. Historically constrained by geography, infrastructure and intermediaries, distribution has been one of the most disruptive areas of automation.

Examples of distribution automation include:

- Standardized shipping containers
- Global logistics networks
- Warehousing and fulfillment systems
- Digital delivery of services and information
- Platform-based marketplaces

In the Automated Economy, distribution becomes **invisible** to the buyer. Speed, reliability and optionality replace physical presence as competitive advantages.

Means of Commerce

Means of commerce defines how buyers discover, evaluate, purchase and receive value.

This system includes:

- Marketing and branding
- Sales models
- Pricing structures
- Contracting and payment
- Customer experience and trust mechanisms

Automation here is often misunderstood as purely digital. In reality, many of the most powerful acquisition automations are **business model innovations**.

The grocery store itself was an automation—removing the need for buyers to negotiate individually with producers. Subscription models automate repeat purchasing and delivery. Marketplaces automate trust and comparison.

AUTOMATION BEYOND TECHNOLOGY

One of the most dangerous misconceptions in modern enterprise strategy is the belief that automation equals technology.

Technology is merely **one expression** of automation.

True economic automation occurs whenever friction is removed from one or more of the three core systems, production, distribution and the means of commerce. Often, this is achieved not through software, but through **re-architected value exchange**.

Consider historical examples:

- The grocery store automated aggregation and access
- The catalog automated discovery and ordering
- The franchise automated brand consistency
- Insurance bundles automated risk distribution
- Subscription pricing automated renewal and retention

None of these required advanced computing to fundamentally automate economic behavior.

The Automated Economy accelerates when business models **invert assumptions** about ownership, access and value delivery.

HYPER-AUTOMATION AND HYPER-PERSONALIZATION

The modern economy is simultaneously:

- **Hyper-automated**—reducing human intervention in execution
- **Hyper-personalized**—increasing relevance to individual buyers

This is not a contradiction. Automation enables personalization by making variability economically viable.

Personalization without automation is cost prohibitive. Automation without personalization is commoditization.

ECONOMIC ERAS AS WAVES OF AUTOMATION

Economic eras do not replace one another instantly. They propagate in **overlapping global waves**, shaped by geography, capital availability, labor structures and political systems.

Agrarian Era

Agrarian economies automated survival. Tools, crop rotation and land ownership structures optimized production for stability rather than growth.

Industrial Era

Industrialization automated scale. Mechanization, factories and standardized labor transformed production and distribution, but often constrained acquisition to mass markets.

Computerized Era

The computerized era automated calculation, planning and coordination. Enterprise Resource Planning (ERP), Manufacturing Resource Planning (MRP) systems and early logistics software optimized internal efficiency more than external responsiveness.

Digital Era

The digital era automated connectivity and choice. Platforms, e-commerce and data analytics shifted power decisively toward buyers.

THE AUTOMATED ECONOMY AS CONVERGENCE

The Automated Economy is the convergence of all prior eras, unified by continuous feedback loops between buyer behavior and enterprise execution. It is not a replacement for the agrarian, industrial, information, or digital eras, but rather the cumulative result of them. Each era introduced a new layer of capability into the economy. The agrarian era established the fundamentals of production and survival through localized labor and seasonal output. The industrial era introduced scale, mechanization and repeatability. The information era increased coordination, planning and visibility across larger and more complex enterprises. The digital era reduced the friction of communication, data exchange and transactional interaction. The Automated Economy emerges when the capabilities of these prior eras are no longer operating in isolation, but are increasingly interconnected and responsive to one another.

What makes this convergence meaningful is the speed and continuity of the connection between demand and response. In earlier eras, buyer behavior influenced the enterprise slowly and often indirectly. Preferences were inferred through lagging sales data, channel feedback, market studies, or delayed operational adjustments. In the Automated Economy, buyer behavior becomes an active and persistent source of operational input. Search activity, purchasing patterns, service interactions, usage behavior and expectation signals continuously inform how enterprises plan, produce, position, distribute and support goods and services. The enterprise is no longer merely reacting to the market in periodic cycles; it is increasingly operating within an ongoing system of sensing, interpreting and responding.

This convergence also means enterprise functions which were once managed separately are becoming more interdependent. Product availability influences customer experience. Customer experience shapes demand patterns. Demand patterns affect supply chain activity. Supply chain performance impacts financial outcomes, labor requirements and service levels. As these interactions become more visible and more immediate, the boundaries between front-office and back-office operations begin to matter less than the quality of coordination across the whole system. The Automated Economy therefore represents not just technological advancement, but a structural shift in how the economy functions—through connected systems, continuous signals and increasingly synchronized execution.

This is the defining characteristic of the Automated Economy: not simply that more work is automated, but that more parts of the economy are operating in relation to one another through shared data, shared signals and shared response mechanisms. Convergence is the point. The economy becomes more integrated across production, distribution, commerce, and service because the signals that guide these activities are flowing with greater speed, precision and continuity than in any prior era. That is what gives the Automated Economy its distinctive power and what makes it a meaningful advancement beyond the Digital Era alone.

DIGITAL ENABLEMENT AS THE ACCELERATION MECHANISM

Acceleration into the Automated Economy does not occur organically for most enterprises. Legacy structures resist change. Fragmentation slows response.

Digital Enablement is the discipline that **unifies intent, execution and feedback** across the enterprise.

THE FIVE UNIFIED BUSINESS SEGMENTS

To operate effectively in the Automated Economy, organizations must align five segments as a single system:

Branding & Marketing

Shapes perception, signals value and attracts demand.

Sales & Commerce

Translates interest into transactions with minimal friction.

Operations & Order Fulfillment

Executes promises reliably, efficiently and at scale.

Customer Engagement

Maintains relevance, trust and ongoing relationship value.

Service Delivery Management

Ensures outcomes, accountability and long-term value realization.

Automation fails when these segments optimize independently. Acceleration occurs when they function as **one adaptive organism**.

THE STRATEGIC IMPLICATION FOR LEADERSHIP

The Automated Economy fundamentally redefines leadership responsibility.

Leaders are no longer stewards of static systems. They are architects of **adaptive capability**.

Competitive advantage now comes from:

- Speed of learning
- Precision of response
- Elasticity of operating models
- Alignment between buyer demand and enterprise action

The organizations that fail in this era will not do so because they lacked technology—but because they failed to **re-design themselves for automation at the system level**.

The Automated Economy does not ask for permission.

It advances wherever friction exists. It rewards those who design for it and punishes those who defend legacy assumptions. Buyers will always migrate toward systems that serve them better.

The only strategic question left for leadership is not *if* they will enter the Automated Economy—but **whether they will lead the transition or be reshaped by it**.

To accelerate growth in the Automated Economy, understanding automation is not enough. Organizations must be **digitally enabled**.

Digital Enablement is the deliberate alignment of strategy, systems, culture and execution to operate at the speed of the Automated Economy. It replaces siloed thinking with integrated capability. It transforms technology from a department into a foundation.

Digitally enabled enterprises move away from legacy models that depend on manual effort, disconnected systems, and delayed insight. They evolve into adaptive, self-optimizing organizations capable of scaling revenue and profitability simultaneously. A self-optimizing organization continuously senses change, learns from signals, adjust workflows and improves outcomes through connected systems and guided human oversight.

This is not optional. It is structural.

The longer an organization delays this shift, the more friction accumulates beneath the surface. Complexity increases. Visibility decreases. Growth slows—not suddenly, but steadily.

Every era presents the same choice, even if it feels different each time:

- Stay the same and attempt to ride it out
- Innovate and adapt to the new reality
- Or be left behind

The Automated Economy is already here. The only question is whether your organization is positioned to accelerate within it—or whether it will be reshaped by those who are.

Digital Enablement is the bridge between the world as it is and the future that is forming.

The remainder of this book exists to show you how to cross it—intentionally, intelligently and fast enough to matter.

The Automated Economy is the convergence of all prior eras, unified by continuous feedback loops between buyer behavior and enterprise execution.

PART THREE

DIGITAL ENABLEMENT

A CEO, COO AND CFO GUIDE TO COMPETING IN THE AUTOMATED ECONOMY

For any company to succeed in the Automated Economy, the company must become digitally enabled. For years, simply using a word such as "digital" often referred to something related to technology. Digital Enablement is not an IT initiative, a transformation program, or initiative to be scheduled between product launches or budget cycles. It is not a collection of technology upgrades, or a department to be created, or a title to be awarded. It is the exact capability that determines whether an enterprise can operate at the pace of buyer expectations, or whether it will be overtaken by competitors who already can.

Digital Enablement is the operating philosophy that determines whether an enterprise can grow revenue, scale operations and make decisions at the speed demanded by modern markets.

In the Automated Economy, value is created by organizations that can:

- Automate at scale without increasing complexity
- Personalize experiences without increasing cost
- Make decisions based on real-time data rather than retrospective reports

The time is now for a clear, executive level understanding of what Digital Enablement is. It is time for us to embrace a clear understanding for why legacy thinking has become structurally limiting and how digitally enabled enterprises are unlocking sustained growth, efficiency and resilience.

Digital Enablement is the intentional design of an enterprise so that technology amplifies human capability rather than constrains it. It is the integration of Hyper-automation, Hyper-personalization and Data-driven decision making into the core fabric of how the business operates. It moves beyond departments, eliminates silos, pushes past hierarchies, organizes disparate systems, and eliminates duplicated work, waste and inefficiency. Digital Enablement creates intelligent, interconnected systems that amplify human judgement and automate routine operations in real time.

A digitally enabled enterprise exhibits three operating principles. These are:

Hyper Automated

Automation is not applied to isolated tasks or departments. It is designed end-to-end across value streams—the end-to-end flows of work through which value is created and delivered to the buyer—so work moves continuously with minimal friction. Hyper-automation eliminates manual handoffs, reduces cycle time and compresses the distance between intent and execution. Human effort is reserved for judgment, creativity and leadership, while repeatable execution is handled by systems.

Hyper Personalized

Customers, partners and employees are treated as individuals, not averages, or simply a transaction. Experiences, offerings, communications and services adapt dynamically based on context, behavior, and intent. This is individualized experience at scale. Buyers no longer compare experiences within a single product category. They compare them against the highest standard they encounter anywhere—from consumer apps to real-time services in their daily lives. Hyper-personalization uses context, behavior and predictive inference to deliver experiences that feel uniquely tailored to the individual without constant human orchestration.

Data-Driven Decisions

Decisions are no longer delayed by reporting cycles or filtered through organizational bias. Data flows in real time, informing both human judgment and autonomous system actions. Data-driven decision making involves collecting, analyzing, and leveraging data to guide strategic and operational choices, ensuring that decisions are grounded in empirical evidence. Digital Enablement uses integrated data infrastructure to eliminate information silos and place accurate, contextual data where it is needed at the moment it is needed. By using statistical models, machine learning and analytics tools, organizations can uncover actionable insights that improve outcomes and reduce risk.

Digital Enablement is not about installing tools. It is about redesigning how value is created. These three principles of Digital Enablement are not independent. They reinforce one another. Together, they accelerate execution, sharpen responsiveness and create a decision advantage over competitors who still rely on legacy thinking and architectural constraints.

THE EVOLUTION FROM LEGACY THINKING TO DIGITAL THINKING

For years, we have trained our enterprises and the people working within them to acquire and use technology in certain ways. Most enterprises are constrained not by technology, but by legacy thought leadership. These are mental models formed in earlier economic eras that no longer align with how value is created today. The challenge is not a lack of technology. The challenge is a corporate mind-set.

Most enterprises are designed on legacy paradigms—command and control hierarchies, departmental silos, human centric static SOPs and value measurement anchored in lagging financial metrics. These structures made sense in eras when time horizons were measured in quarters and annual planning cycles. They do not make sense when buyer expectations shift week to week; information flows instantly and competitive advantage is determined by milliseconds of decision latency—the elapsed time between an event occurring and the organization taking effective action.

Legacy Thought Leadership shapes organizational design, performance evaluation, capital allocation, role definitions and incentive systems. It assumes predictability in an environment that now rewards adaptability. It assumes stability in a landscape defined by acceleration. It assumes human coordination structures can outpace machine-augmented decision cycles. None of these assumptions are true in the Automated Economy.

The evidence is in the market itself. Enterprises that cling to legacy structures experience persistent friction, growth bottlenecks and operational drag. Inefficiencies that once manifested as cost overruns now manifest as lost market share. Data negativity—siloed, inconsistent, delayed—becomes strategic blind spots rather than mere technical problems. Systems that do not speak to one another become operational liabilities. Manual processes that once empowered local control now slow enterprise-wide responsiveness.

The fundamental truth is this: legacy thinking is not neutral. It is a decline.

The executive dilemma is stark: maintaining the status quo is no longer a neutral choice. In the Automated Economy, it is increasingly a fatal one.

Why Legacy Thought Leadership is Now a Constraint

In the Automated Economy, consumer access to information and choice has outpaced most companies' ability to respond.

Buyers compare experiences across industries. A bank loan is measured against e-commerce checkout. A truck fleet service is measured against ride-hail dispatch time. A supplier portal is measured against mobile app speed. Expectations that were once acceptable within a single industry no longer hold when buyers have experienced instant responses in other domains.

This elevated expectation is pervasive:

- Customers expect near-real-time answers, not 48-hour support queues
- They expect experiences to be personalized, not generic
- They expect interactions to be consistent, not fragmented
- They expect operational reliability across channels and stages of engagement

Where product quality and price converge, experience becomes the differentiator. Organizations that cannot deliver frictionless, integrated, personalized engagement become commoditized. Those that can command premium pricing, higher retention, and exponential growth.

The Structural Collapse of Silos

Buyer expectation is not the only force compressing enterprise boundaries. As choice expands, so do interdependencies across production, distribution and commerce.

In legacy models, these functions operated independently. Production planning in one silo. Order fulfillment in another. Finance in another. Marketing in another. Customer service in another. These separations worked when throughput was slow and cycles long. They do not work when choice expands faster than systems can coordinate.

A digitally enabled enterprise does not fracture operations. It integrates them. It creates unified visibility, shared data context and real-time feedback loops. Operations are informed by sales data. Sales are informed by supply chain capacity. Customer engagement is connected to fulfillment performance. Decisions are not sequential. They are simultaneous.

This convergence does not happen by accident. It requires intentional architecture—semantic data layers, unified platforms, automated workflows, real-time analytics. Semantic data layers provide a shared business meaning layer so different systems interpret the same data consistently. A global manufacturer may have their sales team using a client relationship management (CRM) system, operations using an ERP, customer service using a ticketing platform, and finance using its own reporting environment. If each system defines a "customer," "order," "margin," or even "on-time delivery" differently, then leadership meetings become consumed by conflicting numbers instead of decisive action. Sales may report that a major account is growing, operations may believe the account is unprofitable because fulfillment costs are rising, and finance may show delayed cash conversion with no single version of the truth. In that environment, teams do not simply move slower; they begin to work against one another because each function is operating from a different interpretation of reality.

By contrast, a semantic data layer creates shared business meaning across those systems. The enterprise can define, for example, what constitutes a customer, a booked order, a shipped order, a profitable account, or an at-risk customer in one consistent way. Once that is established, automated workflows and real-time analytics can operate with confidence across the business. A pricing change can immediately reflect its impact on demand, fulfillment capacity, service levels, and margin. Instead of debating whose data is correct, leadership can focus on what action to take next. Enterprises that fail to build this architecture experience fragmentation, delayed responses and internal conflict over priorities.

Legacy Thought Leadership constrains organizations at every level—from the boardroom to the forklift operator. It defines how people are organized, how work is performed, and how success is measured, often without questioning whether those constructs still serve the business.

History provides clear lessons:

- Tesla eliminated dealerships, redefining distribution
- Amazon rejected short-term ROI logic to build long-term dominance

These companies did not optimize existing models. They eliminated structural constraints. And they did so by advancing the way they think, progressing thought leadership with acceleration through digitally enabled thinking:

- Networked, outcome-driven leadership
- Value streams replacing functional silos

- Digital-centric methods and procedures
- Real-time, predictive decision systems
- Investment models that prioritize learning and scale

Throughout every era, the enterprise that accelerates wins. The key takeaway is clear: enterprises must fundamentally rethink how organizations are constructed and how value is measured if they want to remain competitive.

DIGITAL ENABLEMENT AND THE AUTOMATED ECONOMY

Economic evolution has always been driven by buyer demand. From bartering to industrialization to digitization, each era increased convenience, speed and choice.

Today, consumers have:

- Instant access to information
- Global communication at zero marginal cost
- Deep visibility into markets and alternatives

In many cases, **consumers now know more about the markets they care about than the companies serving them.**

This asymmetry creates a defining question for leaders: If a department requires 100 people today, how could it be redesigned to operate with 10 tomorrow?

Digital Enablement is the mechanism by which organizations accelerate into this new reality.

Clarity: The First Imperative

Effective Digital Enablement begins with clarity—a clear, concrete agreement about the future state the enterprise must pursue.

This clarity is not high concept or inspirational. It is operational. It answers:

- How will we deliver value faster than competitors?
- How will we compress decision cycles?
- How will we orchestrate systems to act autonomously?
- How will we measure success in real time?
- How will we neutralize latency, friction and blind spots?

Clarity also reveals the strategic choice each enterprise faces: Innovator, Adopter or Implementer. At the center of the Automated Economy is a simple truth: the buyer mindset is that buyers want what they want, when they want it, at the value they are willing to pay.

Industries are disrupted whether organizations choose to participate or not. Every enterprise eventually plays a role within the industry in which they operate. These roles are: Innovator, Adopter or Implementer.

INNOVATOR, ADOPTER OR IMPLEMENTER: A STRATEGIC CHOICE

Enterprises must make a conscious choice about where they will compete. In every era, participants fall into three broad roles:

- **Innovators** create new categories and business models. They redefine expectations. They reshape markets
- **Adopters** refine and scale emerging models
- **Implementers** scale proven innovations. They optimize, standardize and extend reach. Implementers win through efficiency and cost leadership

Before you can decide *how* to invest, you must decide *who you are* in your current competitive context.

Every leadership team tends to misclassify itself. Many claim to be innovators when they are truly adopters. Many claim to be adopters when they are functioning as implementers. And some are implementers but have convinced themselves that implementation is "less strategic."

The question is not what you admire. The question is *what can you execute?*

Innovator

Innovators create new advantages where none existed.

They introduce new customer experiences, new operating models, new value creation mechanisms and in some cases entirely new categories. Innovators are not defined by creativity. They are defined by their ability to absorb uncertainty, finance experimentation and operationalize what works.

Innovators win by shaping the rules of the market—until the market stabilizes enough for adopters to scale the innovation and for implementers to industrialize it.

Adopter

Adopters are the scaling engine of the economy.

They do not need to invent the future to win; they need to recognize it early, adopt it faster than competitors and scale it with discipline. Adopters can dominate markets precisely because they avoid the cost of invention while still capturing the upside of early movement.

In the Automated Economy, adopters often win because speed of adoption, integration and execution matters more than originality.

Implementer

Implementers win through operational excellence and repeatability.

They industrialize capability. They transform "innovations" into stable systems that work every day, at scale, under constraints. They deliver reliability, cost efficiency, compliance, governance and predictable performance.

In a converging world where production, distribution, and commerce must be unified, implementers can become extraordinarily powerful because they know how to turn complexity into consistency.

Each of these roles is valid. Each serves a distinct purpose, and each has a legitimate place in the market. But they are not interchangeable. An enterprise cannot fully operate as all three at once without creating internal contradiction. At some point, every enterprise must choose which role it will primarily play. These roles are mutually exclusive at the strategic level.

Attempting to be all three leads to dilution of focus, capability, and market identity.

Electric vehicles provide a clear example:

- Tesla and Lucid disrupted the market at the premium tier
- Mass-market players entered later as adopters of the original business model
- Many brands are now implementing a mass production strategy fine-tuned by the innovators and adopters and driving unit costs down rapidly

Tesla and Lucid acted as innovators in the electric vehicle industry, creating category standards. And while others entered later as adopters copying the business model, several others have entered the marketplace eventually achieving scale through cost-focused models.

When an executive team misclassifies its organization type, it misallocates capital, time and leadership attention.

- An implementer that invests like an innovator will burn time and credibility
- An adopter that invests like an implementer will lose speed
- An innovator that invests like an adopter will lose its edge

This choice is not a workshop exercise with opinions and politics. It must be a structured assessment with evidence, constraints and market realities—often facilitated by a strategic partner who can create neutral alignment.

All enterprises must decide which role to play. Then design systems, metrics and rewards that align to that choice. The lesson is not to copy strategies, but to choose deliberately. Not every company has to be an innovator. But every company must decide whether it will innovate, adopt early or implement at scale.

Focus: Delivering on the Buyer Promise

Digital Enablement requires focus. Focus is not about reducing activity. It is about aligning activity with strategic clarity. Previously, we introduced the five unified business segments.

The enterprises who are achieving success and sustainability in the Automated Economy have a Hyper Focus on these five unified business segments within the enterprise. **Every function must operate in alignment with buyer expectations hyper focused in these five segments**:

- Branding and marketing must communicate relevance and connection
- Sales and commerce must convert interest into action without friction
- Operations and fulfillment must scale with precision and predictability
- Customer engagement must be continuous and integrated
- Service delivery management must be transparent and automated

These segments are the vital areas of the business needing to operate effectively within the Automated Economy and supersede any silo, department or hierarchy. They must work together across the segments to most effectively deliver on the buyer promise. Enterprise systems must remove friction, not create it. When these segments are working in alignment, revenue growth is accelerated, operation execution is frictionless and real-time operational data and analytics are empowering informed decisions across every segment. Digitally enabled enterprises have automated workflows that eliminate manual handoffs and the enterprise is now able to predictably plan and anticipate customer needs. These further enable scalable on-demand infrastructure to rapidly adapt to usage patterns, not simply traditional fixed schedules.

- When Branding anticipates demand…
- When Sales convert without friction…
- When Operations executes predictively…
- When Engagement extends value continuously…
- When Service governs trust transparently…

Then:

- The enterprise becomes synchronized
- Data flows across segments
- Insights inform every decision
- Infrastructure adapts in real time
- The buyer experience feels effortless

Segment One: Branding and Marketing: Architecting Attention and Intent

Branding and Marketing in the Automated Economy is no longer campaign driven, it is intelligence driven.

The modern enterprise must possess a deep understanding of buyer behavior and intent. Not demographics. Not assumptions. Real behavioral data.

Digitally enabled marketing systems continuously capture engagement signals—search patterns, content interaction, product browsing, purchase history, response timing. These signals form predictive models that reveal not only what customers have done, but what they are likely to do next.

Intent becomes measurable.

Presence, therefore, must follow attention. Customer attention is fragmented across platforms, devices and digital ecosystems. Enterprises that rely on habitual channel allocation lose relevance. Digitally enabled organizations dynamically allocate resources where attention truly resides—guided by live performance analytics.

Brand alignment must also be authentic and measurable. In a transparent environment, values are not marketing slogans; they are scrutinized behaviors. Sentiment monitoring, social listening, and feedback analytics surface perception shifts in real time. The brand becomes governed by insight rather than assumption.

Finally, engagement must be personalized, timely and relevant. Automation enables behavior-triggered communication, predictive offer sequencing, AI-curated content and dynamic messaging flows. Engagement becomes contextual. The message meets the buyer at the moment of decision.

When Branding and Marketing operate digitally, they do not generate noise.

They generate alignment.

Segment Two: Sales and Commerce: Eliminating Friction Between Desire and Transaction

In traditional organizations, sales is a funnel.

In digitally enabled enterprises, sales is a fluid journey.

Customers move across channels seamlessly—mobile to desktop, in-store to digital, social to search. The enterprise must move with them. Unified customer identity across channels eliminates repetition. Shopping carts persist. Payment systems integrate smoothly. Inventory visibility is real time.

Conversion becomes frictionless.

Personalized buying paths adapt dynamically based on predictive modeling. Product recommendations, bundled offers, financing options and upsell opportunities are informed by behavioral data. The enterprise anticipates needs before they are articulated.

Repeat purchasing must be effortless. Subscription models, auto-replenishment, stored preferences and one-click reorders transform loyalty into convenience. Friction is removed not only from acquisition—but from retention.

Service availability must also be on-demand. Order confirmations, shipment tracking, automated issue resolution and self-service portals ensure that commerce does not end at checkout.

In the Automated Economy, the transaction must feel immediate, intuitive and seamless.

Anything less introduces risk.

Segment Three: Operations and Order Fulfillment: Turning Execution into Predictive Precision

Operations is where strategy becomes reality.

And in digitally enabled enterprises, Operations is no longer reactive.

Real-time operational visibility becomes foundational. Unified dashboards integrate supply chain data, production capacity, inventory levels, logistics tracking and delivery status. Leaders see what is happening—not what happened.

Predictive planning replaces crisis management. AI-driven forecasting anticipates demand spikes, supplier disruption, equipment failure, and labor constraints. Risk avoidance becomes systematic rather than heroic.

Infrastructure must scale on demand. Cloud-native systems and elastic capacity models allow organizations to expand or contract based on usage patterns—not fixed schedules. Cost structures align with real demand.

Most critically, execution must be integrated end-to-end. Procurement, manufacturing, distribution, and delivery systems communicate continuously. Manual handoffs are eliminated. Workflows are automated across platforms.

When Operations is digitally enabled, fulfillment becomes precise, predictable and scalable.

The enterprise delivers what it promises—consistently.

Segment 4: Customer Engagement: Extending Value Beyond the Transaction

In the Automated Economy, the sale is not the finish line.

It is the starting point of relationship.

Digitally enabled organizations gather product usage insight in real time. Connected platforms reveal feature adoption, engagement frequency, friction points and customer behavior patterns. This intelligence fuels proactive outreach.

Community-driven interaction strengthens brand equity. Online ecosystems, peer forums, user-generated content, and ambassador networks amplify credibility. The enterprise becomes a platform for shared experience.

Continuous value creation replaces episodic communication. Automated updates, personalized education, predictive renewal reminders and usage optimization suggestions ensure that value delivery never stops.

Marketplace feedback loops close the gap between customer voice and product evolution. Reviews, surveys, behavioral analytics and sentiment modeling feed directly into improvement cycles. Learning accelerates across segments.

Customer Engagement, when digitally enabled, compounds lifetime value.

Segment 5: Service Delivery Management: Governing Trust at Scale

Trust is sustained through execution discipline.

Digitally enabled Service Delivery Management embeds transparency into governance.

Performance metrics, compliance dashboards and audit trails are visible and actionable.

Maintenance and process oversight become automated. Preventative maintenance systems, automated updates, workflow orchestration and policy enforcement reduce downtime and human error.

Employees must also be enabled continuously. AI-assisted tools, real-time performance dashboards, automated knowledge systems and on-demand training elevate human capability. Repetitive work declines. Strategic contribution rises.

Communication must be always-on and omni-channel. Customers and employees engage through unified platforms—chatbots, AI assistants, live agents—operating in seamless coordination.

Service Delivery Management ensures that promises made by marketing, sales and operations are upheld consistently.

It protects reputation at scale.

Execution: Architecting the Digitally Enabled Enterprise

Digital Enablement is not a project. It is an enterprise architecture. To move beyond legacy mindsets, leaders need a modern execution model.

Effective Digital Enablement requires integration across four foundational dimensions:

- Organization. Break down silos. Enable cross-functional teams. Connect decision rights to outcomes. Replace rigid hierarchies and departmentalized silos with digitally enabled organizational structures designed around value creation.

- Methods and procedures. Replace static SOPs with adaptive workflows that respond to real-time data signals. Shift from human-centric SOPs to digital-centric methods that scale with demand.
- Systems and technology. Transition from fragmented applications to integrated enterprise platforms that function like a living system—adaptive, responsive and mission-oriented.
- Metrics and KPIs. Replace lagging indicators with real-time measures of velocity, automation coverage, exception rates and customer experience outcomes. Move from static reports to autonomous, Data-driven decision systems capable of acting in real time.

In the digitally enabled enterprise, systems do not simply report. They act.

In digitally enabled architecture:

- Automated workflow systems eliminate manual handoffs and reduce cycle times by enabling straight-through processing, meaning work that moves initiation to completion without manual intervention except by exception
- Intelligent analytics platforms transform raw data into actionable insights that drive proactive decision-making rather than reactive responses
- Scalable technology architectures grow with business demands without requiring complete system overhauls
- Integrated data infrastructure ensures every function works from the same accurate information simultaneously, eliminating blind spots and alignment gaps

This architecture unlocks enterprise capacity not by scaling harder, but by scaling smarter—through real-time responsiveness rather than static predictability.

The Reality of the Automated Economy

In the Automated Economy:

- Buyers expect personalized responses within seconds, not hours
- Markets reward organizations that can respond faster than competitors
- Decisions must be data-informed and immediate
- Operational capacity is measured by responsiveness, not by headcount
- The new growth model is fewer handoffs, more output. Headcount growth is a legacy metric. Outcomes are the new metric that matters.

Firms that become proficient with Digital Enablement compete on value, experience and outcomes rather than price alone. They command pricing premiums, retain customers more effectively and drive growth at higher velocity than competitors who remain anchored to legacy structures.

Digital Enablement is not a tagline. It is the outcome of deliberate enterprise architecture. It is the decision to operate at Automated Economy scale. It is the choice to synchronize Hyper-automation, Hyper-personalization and Data-driven decision making across every function.

Silos are a choice. Resistance is a choice. Remaining unchanged is a choice.

But in the Automated Economy, hesitation is not stability. It is drift toward irrelevance.

Digital Enablement is the capability that allows an enterprise to thrive amidst choice expansion, converging business models and learning models that evolve faster than organizational inertia.

Therefore, you must become digitally enabled.

The challenge is not understanding this—it is executing it. Most organizations already sense the need to change, but struggle to translate that awareness into coordinated action. Internal teams are often constrained by legacy structures, competing priorities, and limited visibility into where friction truly exists.

This is where external perspective becomes critical. The right partner can compress years of experimentation into months of focused execution—aligning leadership, identifying where to start, and building the architecture required to scale with precision.

Effective enterprises do not attempt this alone. Strategic partners accelerate learning, reduce risk, and compress time-to-value. They enable elevated thinking and help to accelerate outcomes.

The Choice is Real

Digital Enablement is not optional. Enterprises will either accelerate into the Automated Economy or be rendered irrelevant by those that do.

Some organizations are already digitally enabled. Many are beginning the journey. The opportunity for you is to decide to become digitally enabled. It is a choice you can make or allow the market to do it for you.

Digital Enablement is not about installing tools. It is about redesigning how value is created.

PART FOUR

DIGITAL ENABLEMENT CALL TO ACTION—NOW IS THE TIME TO ENGAGE

This book is our effort to inspire you to elevate your thinking, and to engage in an effort to accelerate into the Automated Economy. Our journey in sharing within this book has been a deliberate walk through in helping you to see a reality reshaping every enterprise, every industry, and every leader's responsibility. We have taken this step to share what is taking place in our marketplace, not to describe a trend, promote a technology, or react to a moment. It has been written to reveal a pattern—a pattern that has repeated across centuries and is now accelerating beyond the tolerance of legacy systems.

We began with a simple story; we are not the lighthouse, yet have several moments each day on a collision course towards one.

We proceeded by introducing a foundational truth: economies do not move because technologies emerge. They move because buyers choose. Across agrarian villages, industrial cities, digital marketplaces, and now algorithmic ecosystems, the prime mover has always been the same—the buyer's desire to obtain what they want, when they want it, at the value they are willing to exchange. That timeless equation sits underneath every macro disruption in history. Technology amplifies it. Business models respond to it. Learning systems chase it. But the accelerant is always the buyer.

From that foundation, we explored the first force of macro disruption: the rapid expansion of choices. Choice expansion is not a side effect of innovation; it is the initiating destabilizer of markets. As options multiply, switching costs decline. Loyalty weakens. Comparison becomes instantaneous. What once required effort, time, or proximity now occurs in seconds. Buyers gain transparency and leverage. And with that leverage, expectations reset.

Abundance, however, does not create clarity. It creates complexity. When buyers are overwhelmed by optionality, they seek simplification. This is why platforms, aggregators and ecosystems rise to power. They do not merely offer products. They orchestrate discovery. They reduce cognitive friction. They control the flow of decision-making. As we examined throughout this book, power migrates from producers to orchestrators when choice expands beyond human processing capacity. The strategic question for leaders therefore shifts from "What do we sell?" to "How do buyers find, compare, and decide?" Organizations built for scarcity struggle in abundance because their structures assume stability, predictable demand, and linear journeys. Choice expansion invalidates those assumptions first. Everything else reacts.

The second force we examined was the evolution of business models. Business model change is not a creative exercise; it is a structural response to buyer power. As buyers gain alternatives, transparency and speed, legacy compromises become unacceptable. Ownership increasingly feels like friction rather than value. Delayed fulfillment feels like incompetence rather than patience. Opaque pricing feels like manipulation rather than tradition. As a result, the architecture of value creation, delivery, monetization and risk allocation must evolve simultaneously.

We explored the shift from goods-centric to outcome-centric models, from transactional revenue to recurring value streams, from product resale to Product-as-a-Service enablement. Manufacturing does not disappear in this shift; it is repositioned. It becomes a means of enabling service promises rather than an endpoint of value. Revenue recognition changes. Risk migrates. Lifetime value replaces point-of-sale margins as the dominant economic logic. FedEx did not merely accelerate mail delivery;

it monetized certainty and time compression. Amazon did not merely digitize bookstores; it normalized immediacy, optionality, and frictionless acquisition. In each case, the new model made prior trade-offs obsolete and permanently reset buyer expectations.

We also confronted the executive blind spots that often delay this evolution: protecting legacy margins, digitizing inefficiency rather than redesigning value and defending industry conventions with the dangerous refrain, "That's not how our industry works." Macro disruption does not respect industry boundaries. Buyers do not compare experiences within silos; they compare them against the best standard they encounter anywhere. The enterprises that succeed in this environment are not necessarily the most innovative in technology; they are the most intentional in redesigning around buyer outcomes.

The third force we examined was the evolution of learning models. This force is less visible, but no less disruptive. For over a century, education systems assumed that knowledge could be front-loaded before work began. Degrees preceded responsibility. Mastery preceded execution. Stability was assumed. That assumption has collapsed. Skill half-lives have shortened dramatically. Tools evolve quarterly. Business models pivot annually. Competitive advantages erode quickly. In this environment, learning detached from execution becomes strategically insufficient.

We traced the movement from credential-based legitimacy to capability-based relevance. From episodic training to embedded, real-time learning. From static content to adaptive systems that surface guidance at the moment of decision. The enterprise itself is becoming the primary learning institution because traditional education cannot update at the velocity required by modern markets. Learning velocity has emerged as a competitive advantage. Organizations that integrate learning into workflows, measure adaptability and reduce time-to-competence will outpace those that treat training as overhead.

These three forces—expanding choices, evolving business models and accelerating learning systems—converge into what we defined as the Automated Economy. This economy is not a prediction of the future; it is the structural maturation of patterns that have been compounding for decades. Automation has always powered scale. The plow automated survival. The factory automated production. The computer automated calculation. The internet automated connectivity. The Automated Economy automates responsiveness. For the first time in history, economic systems can align with buyer intent in near real time across global markets.

Automation in this era extends beyond machinery or software. It includes business model design, organizational structure, decision-making architecture, personalization engines and feedback loops. The modern economy is simultaneously Hyper-automated and Hyper-personalized. This is not a contradiction. Automation makes personalization economically viable at scale. Without automation, personalization is cost- prohibitive. Without personalization, automation leads to commoditization. The competitive advantage lies in synchronizing the two.

The structural implication of this convergence is clear: enterprises must become digitally enabled. Digital Enablement is not digitization. It is not an IT initiative or a technology upgrade. It is the intentional redesign of enterprise architecture to operate at the speed of buyer behavior. A digitally enabled enterprise is Hyper-automated across value streams, Hyper-personalized in its interactions, and driven by real-time data rather than retrospective reporting.

We examined how this requires the alignment of five unified business segments:

- Branding and Marketing
- Sales and Commerce
- Operations and Fulfillment
- Customer Engagement
- Service Delivery Management

When various departments within an enterprise operate as independent silos, friction accumulates and latency increases. When an enterprise chooses to focus on these five key business segments and are designed to operate as an integrated system, the enterprise becomes synchronized. Brand anticipates demand. Sales and commerce are converting without friction. Operations executes predictively. Engagement compounds lifetime value. Service governs trust transparently. Data flows across the organization. Insights inform decisions in real time. Infrastructure adapts dynamically. The buyer experience feels effortless.

Throughout this book, we also addressed the presence of Legacy Thought Leadership within all of us, and how we need to find others; mentors, coaches, trusted advisors, external partners, to help us eliminate it. Command-and-control hierarchies, departmental silos, static SOPs and lagging financial metrics were designed for slower eras. They are structurally limiting in an environment where expectations shift weekly and decision latency is measured in milliseconds. Legacy thinking is not neutral; it creates decline. In the Automated Economy, maintaining the status quo is not stability. It is drift toward irrelevance.

Finally, we confronted the strategic choice every enterprise must make. In every era, participants fall into three roles: innovators who redefine markets, adopters who refine and scale emerging models, and implementers who optimize and extend proven innovations. Each role is valid, but attempting to occupy all three creates dilution. The lesson is not that every company must disrupt its industry. The lesson is that every company must decide deliberately how it will compete within structural acceleration.

Our summary is intended to help you quickly capture and act to get engaged. It is a chance to take action. It is a recap of what we have methodically established. The pattern is clear. Choice will continue expanding. Business models will continue evolving. Learning systems will continue accelerating. Automation will continue advancing wherever friction exists. The Automated Economy will not pause to accommodate legacy comfort.

The only variable left is design.

Where you go from here depends on whether you treat these forces as temporary turbulence or as structural inevitability. Enterprises that design around buyer outcomes, embed automation across systems, institutionalize learning velocity and synchronize their value streams will accelerate. Those that defend outdated architecture will be reshaped by those who do not.

We have covered the pattern, the forces, the shifts and the architecture required to respond. This book is a map, not a prediction. The Automated Economy is not approaching. It is here. And leadership in this era is defined not by preservation of the past, but by intentional design for what is structurally unfolding.

Understanding the pattern is one thing.

Architecting your enterprise around it is another.

Throughout this book, we have made one idea unmistakably clear: the Automated Economy is structural. It is not a marketing cycle. It is not a technology upgrade window. It is not a transformation initiative you can phase in when time allows. It is a design of how value is created, delivered, monetized, and learned.

And design at this scale requires more than insight.

It requires execution discipline.
It requires architectural clarity.
It requires cross-functional alignment.
It requires leadership acceleration.
It requires measurable outcomes.

Most importantly, it requires an external perspective strong enough to challenge legacy assumptions without being constrained by them. The ability to get outside oneself and see what is needed on a consistent basis.

Becoming digitally enabled is challenging not because the technology does not exist. The technology exists. The data exists. The platforms exist. What most organizations lack is unified clarity, strategic focus and visibility to accelerate—clarity about where friction truly lives, clarity about what must be redesigned versus optimized, and clarity about how to align leadership, systems, and execution around the buyer promise. Strategic focus for what and where to spend the time digitally enabling to have the greatest impact on your enterprise. And the visibility to ensure sustainable acceleration continues.

This is where partnership matters.

In periods of structural acceleration, the most successful enterprises do not isolate themselves. They surround themselves with partners who can compress learning curves, neutralize blind spots, and move with the urgency the market demands. They recognize that transformation delayed is opportunity surrendered.

As an executive, take a moment and consider:

- Clarify what kind of organization you are in your market
- Determine your Digital Enablement maturity with brutal honesty
- Decide, as an executive team, what you will invest—and why—so you can outpace competitors rather than react to them

To do this well, you need more than consensus. You need clarity.

And clarity usually requires a strategic partner.

Now the question is whether you will act to gain strategic clarity—or react under pressure.

Because the market will not pause.

The buyer will not pause.

And competitors who achieve unified intent faster than you will define the new standards your organization must then chase.

Very few partners will align your enterprise end-to-end around growth. Find a partner who will help you get aligned and accelerate into the automated economy.

The reality is simple: Digital Enablement without growth is optimization. And optimization without alignment is fragility.

We began our book on our journey together with an Overview—You Can't Even See It!

This is your inflection point.

Now you can see it. What will you do about it?

We'd love to help you see further; connect with us at Cooperative Computing for your discovery call.

25 EXECUTIVE TAKEAWAYS FOR BECOMING DIGITALLY ENABLED

1. Your biggest risk isn't poor execution—it's outdated thinking

   Most organizations fail because their mental models lag reality, not because their teams lack capability.

2. You are already falling behind—you just can't see it yet

   Irrelevance happens gradually through decision latency and unseen friction, not sudden collapse.

3. The buyer—not your strategy—is the true driver of your business

   Markets don't move because of innovation—they move because buyers choose differently.

4. All strategy must answer one equation

   What do buyers want?

   When do they want it?

   What value will they accept?

   Everything else is secondary.

5. Digital enablement is not about technology

   It is about aligning people, processes, systems, and data to operate at the speed of demand.

6. Technology is now horizontal—not a department

   If digital lives in IT, your organization is structurally misaligned.

7. Silos are the primary enemy of speed

   Fragmented functions = fragmented decisions = slow execution = lost market share.

8. Your organization is likely optimizing departments, not the enterprise

   Local efficiency does not equal global performance.

9. Choice expansion is the earliest warning signal of disruption

   When customers suddenly have more options, your model is already under pressure.

10. You are no longer competing on product—you're competing on decision experience

    The winner is the company that helps buyers choose faster and easier.

11. Business model innovation is not optional—
    it's structural

    If buyer power increases, your business model must evolve or be rejected.

12. Ownership is declining—outcomes are winning

    Customers increasingly want:

    access over ownership

    results over products

13. If you digitize a broken model, you accelerate failure

    Automation without redesign = faster irrelevance.

14. Your biggest blind spot is protecting yesterday's success

    Legacy margins, systems, and habits are often what block tomorrow's growth.

15. Speed of learning is now a competitive advantage

    Organizations that learn faster than change outperform those that plan better.

16. Training is no longer separate from work

    The highest-performing companies embed learning directly into execution.

17. You are not competing on headcount—you are competing on responsiveness

    Modern performance =

    fewer people + better systems + faster decisions

18. Automation is not about replacing people

    It's about removing friction from delivering value at scale.

19. The Automated Economy is already here

    This is not future-state thinking—it is current structural reality.

20. Growth now comes from alignment, not expansion

    More people, tools, or processes won't fix misalignment—they amplify it.

21. Every company must choose its role: Innovator, Adopter, or Implementer

    Trying to be all three creates:

    confusion

    poor capital allocation

    weak execution

22. Decision latency is your hidden cost center

    The longer it takes to decide, the more value you lose—silently.

23. Your real competitor may not be in your industry

    Buyers compare you to the best experience they've had anywhere.

24. Digital enablement requires redesign, not improvement

    This is not optimization—it is architectural change.

25. Doing nothing is not neutral—it is decline

    In the Automated Economy, standing still means:

    increasing friction
    decreasing relevance
    eventual displacement

ABOUT THE AUTHORS

DAVID KRAMER

David Kramer is the Founder, owner and Chief Operating Officer of Cooperative Computing and a recognized innovator in digital enablement. He is also the chief architect for Digital Enablement, and has worked delivering unmatched business results with organizations for four decades. His career is rooted in a passion for building systems that bring clarity, speed and intelligence to how organizations operate in an increasingly complex and automated world.

David began his career serving in the United States Air Force, where he developed a disciplined, mission-first approach to problem-solving, leadership and execution. That foundation continues to shape his work today—bringing precision, accountability and a systems-oriented mindset to every engagement.

With deep expertise in cloud architecture, software development and enterprise systems, David has led the design and implementation of digital platforms that unify data, streamline operations and enable real-time decision-making. He is a strong advocate for moving beyond traditional digital transformation efforts toward true digital enablement—where technology, data and processes are fully aligned to support business outcomes.

As a thought leader, David focuses on helping organizations reimagine how they operate by connecting fragmented systems, activating data across the enterprise and introducing intelligent automation at scale. His work empowers companies to evolve from reactive, manual environments into proactive, digitally enabled enterprises built for performance, scalability and sustained growth.

BRENT SNYDER

Brent Snyder is owner and Chief Executive Officer for Cooperative Computing and a growth-focused leader passionate about helping individuals and organizations unlock their full potential in an increasingly automated world. In his career, Brent works with founders, leadership teams, private equity partners and professional athletes to scale organizations and build high-performing teams that consistently outperform competitors.

Brent leverages decades of high performance leadership ranging from his time in the NFL to becoming one of the leaders in the global thought leadership organization of what is Franklin-Covey today, to bring a unique blend of strategic leadership, commercial acumen, and operational discipline. He believes that greatness is not accidental—it is engineered through clarity, focus, and the right operating model. His work centers on helping leaders move beyond incremental improvement to achieve step-change performance by modernizing how their businesses operate.

At the core of Brent's philosophy is a commitment to inspiring teams to think bigger, move faster, and execute with purpose.

He champions the idea that in the automated economy, sustainable success belongs to organizations that embrace change, leverage data intelligently, and empower their people through technology.

In his leadership at Cooperative Computing, Brent helps enterprises become digitally enabled—aligning strategy, systems, and execution to accelerate growth, increase efficiency, and create lasting enterprise value.

Find a partner who will help you get aligned and accelerate into the automated economy.

The reality is simple: Digital Enablement without growth is optimization. And optimization without alignment is fragility.

ABOUT COOPERATIVE COMPUTING

Cooperative Computing (C|C) is your digital enablement partner helping growth-focused organizations accelerate into the automated economy. By aligning strategy, data, technology, and execution, C|C enables enterprises to grow revenue, operate more efficiently and make data-driven decisions.

Through C|C's Digital Enablement approach, the firm helps organizations Hyper-automate business processes, Hyper-personalize customer experience and integrate systems to activate data-driven decisions. This creates a more connected, agile, and scalable operating model—allowing leadership teams to make better decisions, improve performance across functions, and deliver stronger business outcomes.

With a focus on measurable impact, C|C partners with its clients to transform complexity into clarity, enabling them to accelerate growth and lead with confidence in a rapidly evolving digital landscape with visibility.